"There are sacred moments when life ca [DØ445705]
tiful mystery. Suddenly everything feel.
You want to weep and cheer at the same time. You come away
empowered, fully alive. Timothy sets you down in these moments. Get caught up in them and watch yourself come to life."

—Lacey Sturm, platinum-selling musician and author
of *The Reason: How I Discovered a Life Worth Living*

"Timothy Willard is quickly becoming one of my favorite writers. His poetic words and soul-reaching insights leave me longing
for more: more beauty, more depth, more *Jesus*, which is exactly
what this book offers. If you're aching to see the face of God, if
you're asking to be brought into deeper relationship, if you're
longing for more, let Tim's words help usher you in."

—Sarah Mae, coauthor of *Desperate: Hope for
the Mom Who Needs to Breathe*

"One of the great needs I see for leaders is continued spiritual
growth—the kind that goes deep and fosters intimacy with God.
In *Longing for More*, the reader finds spiritual respite and guidance in insights that point directly to God."

—Brad Lomenick, former director of Catalyst
and author of *The Catalyst Leader: 8 Essentials
for Becoming a Change Maker*

"Timothy Willard has a chance to be the Oswald Chambers to
a new generation. He has a gift to release the power of devotion
that shakes our complacency, exposes our self-righteousness,
and triggers a fresh appetite for the heart of God."

—Dr. Stephen R. Graves, organizational strategist,
theologian, and author of *From Concept to Scale: Creating
a Gospel-Minded Organization*

"In *The Voyage of the Dawn Treader*, C. S. Lewis describes
water so sweet and the Lamb on the shore. In *Longing for More*,

Timothy Willard, a spiritual writer gifted beyond his peers and wise beyond his years, has drawn sweet draughts to quench our thirst and held up visions of the Lamb to inspire our pilgrimage."

—Simon Ponsonby, teaching pastor at St. Aldates Church and author of *More: How You Can Have More of the Spirit When You Already Have Everything in Christ*

"'Set your minds on things above, not on earthly things,' Paul wrote in Colossians. In *Longing for More*, Tim Willard masterfully weaves the heavenly and scriptural perspective of things above with authentic and relatable stories of life here below. One can't help but recalibrate the inner spirit man onto an upward facing trajectory. Thoughtful, encouraging, and insightful, this book is more than just good reading, it's a daily challenge for greater living."

—Logan Wolfram, executive director of Allume and author of LoganWolfram.com

LONGING FOR MORE

LONGING FOR MORE

daily reflections
on finding God
in the rhythms of life

timothy willard

BETHANY HOUSE PUBLISHERS
a division of Baker Publishing Group
Minneapolis, Minnesota

Published by Bethany House Publishers
11400 Hampshire Avenue South
Bloomington, Minnesota 55438
www.bethanyhouse.com

Bethany House Publishers is a division of
Baker Publishing Group, Grand Rapids, Michigan

Printed in the United States of America

Library of Congress Cataloging-in-Publication Data
Willard, Timothy D.
    Longing for more : daily reflections on finding God in the rhythms of life /
Timothy Willard.
        pages cm
    Includes bibliographical references.
    Summary: "Thoughtful daily reflections on how to live a passionate faith amidst everyday life, infused with timeless wisdom from historic Christians"—Provided by publisher.
    ISBN 978-0-7642-1205-5 (pbk. : alk. paper)
    1. Devotional literature. 2. Spiritual life—Christianity—Meditations.
3. Christian life—Meditations. I. Title.
BV4832.3.W53 2014
242'.2—dc23   2014018232

Cover design by Brand Navigation

Author is represented by Christopher Ferebee

14   15   16   17   18   19   20   7   6   5   4   3   2   1

For Whitie,
my father and friend.
Your silent pursuit of Christ hastened mine.

"You must sit down," says Love, "and taste my meat."
So I did sit and eat.[1]

George Herbert

Contents

Contents

Contents

God Rhythms

I wrote this book over the course of two years. It began in the form of private emails to the fellows of Praxis, an entrepreneurial incubator program for founders of social justice organizations. In my service to the fellows, I wrote weekly devotional emails crafted to inspire, challenge, and engender transparency among those in the program. I wanted the writing to reflect the rhythms of daily life but also point to the heavens, to God.

I enjoyed exploring these "God rhythms" so much that I continued to send the emails even after the fellows completed the program; the little pieces enhanced my own times of quiet study and prayer with the Lord Jesus as well. And so, nearly two years later, I am not finishing per se, but bottling them all up for you, expanding some and shortening others.

Why God rhythms? Because life is anything but formulaic. Though I try to implement systems to help organize my time and relationships, these life buckets tend to mix and gel, clash and explode. I experience life like you do, in the whirlwind of reality's rhythms.

But I do not despair in the whirlwind. Instead, I look to its creator, the author of life, the poet of the universe who holds the ebbing and flowing of life like a valley holds its rivers and streams and trees: in the beautiful cadence of balance. The storms interrupt, the rains nourish, the sunlight quickens, the fires purge, and the seasons create a cycle of anticipation. We are always looking to the daffodils, to the picnics, to the harvest parties, to the Christmas trees.

Though we each pass through the same stages of life, our experiences are quite different and yet mysteriously the same. My sisters finished college in four years, but it took me fourteen years, after taking nearly a decade off to pursue music in a band. Our life rhythms, though intermingled, beamed a unique beauty—same, yet different.

How does God weave himself into your life? Does he offer you a list of guidelines to help you from Point A to Point B? Or does he tangle himself into you with a cadence unique to you and specific to him? Everyone who has lived knows life is more like a tangle of rhythms—fugue-like—painful at times, painfully wonderful at others.

Seeking Cadence

The format of this book reflects my own interaction with the Scriptures: focusing on a passage, singling out a verse, reflecting on what the Word is saying and how I can apply it to my life. But do not look for little application points. At times the reflection will not button up nicely, which is quite fine with me. The spiritual life does not turn on and off each day. Rather, it ebbs and flows in a rhythmic dance. Some days I wake up angry for no reason—I need Christ, and quickly! But I do not always find answers. I do, however, find comfort. Sometimes I even pray the same prayer each day: "Lord Jesus, give me strength for this day!" Repetition and rhythm—this is our collective "everyday."

As you will see, I have divided this book into "Weeks." Though the overall layout of the weeks generally aligns with the church calendar, starting in January, you can really begin reading any time of the year. Whether you purchase the book midyear, or just want to jump around to topics you'd like to explore at certain times, the structure is there to suit your needs. Each week includes a writing for each working day, totaling five days. The weekends, I leave to you. I know my rhythm changes on most weekends. I may ride my mountain bike as my quiet time or Sabbath with my family, simply enjoying one another; and to me, this is the deepest part of my worship. You will notice I offer Day 3 as simply a prayer day in that I do not provide you with a verse and a reflection. Instead, I have written reflective prayers. This reveals how I myself feel by Wednesday: in need of nothing else but prayer and strength.

You will spend an entire week focusing on one topic, such as joy or wonder. I hope this provides some continuity to the week for you. I enjoy sitting on an idea or topic for more than just a day.

Every twelfth week I present what I call "The Long Pause." This is a longer piece written for you to reflect on during the week. I have included a brief reflection section with these pieces so that you can be thinking about it the whole week, and maybe even discuss it with a friend or small group. Take advantage of the Long Pause and incorporate a similar pause into your schedule—change things up, evaluate what is working personally or professionally or scholastically for you, unplug for some real time off the grid.

The final two weeks of the year I have left off. Instead, I have included a longer piece as a reflection for the Christmas/New Year holidays. I know many people take vacation during this time, meeting with friends and family, so I wanted to reflect this rhythm in the book. Remember, don't feel pushed into a structure that isn't working for you. If you want to read a more seasonal reflection in July, then by all means! Take these last two weeks to reflect on this piece included and also on your spiritual goals for next year. And, please, spend time with those who love you—that is what makes this time of year so special.

The Fingerprints of Me

Throughout I have included quotes from some of my favorite writers: many theologians, some fiction authors, and some poets. I have deliberately not gone fishing for a "good quote," so as not to have so many quotes from so many authors that your head spins. The quotes you will encounter emerge from my own study and are top of mind for me as I consider a topic or verse.

I do not spend time in a myriad of writers for my quiet time. I have a handful I find helpful, inspiring, and challenging. You will discover my favorites with ease. I do not apologize for the likes of C. S. Lewis and Søren Kierkegaard popping up everywhere. In my opinion, we need to mine the greats. You could spend two years digging into Kierkegaard's beautiful *Works of Love*. Also, please keep in mind that at the time of the writing I was knee-deep reading for a doctorate in theology, studying beauty in the works of C. S. Lewis.

A Journey Together

Finally, I encourage you to pray before each reading. Be careful not to approach this little devotional book as the Word itself— that is to say, do not use it as a replacement for quality time in the Scriptures. This collection merely contains my reflections on the God rhythms I experience in my life. Use them to supplement your own study, your own time of quiet, and your own prayer time.

It humbles me to think of you picking up this book to use as an aid in cultivating your spiritual life. I realize your time is precious, and I look forward to spending it with you.

I have prayed for you as I have written these short pieces. I think of myself as your brother in Christ, and I have tried to write in the same way I would write a note or discuss something with my flesh-and-blood brothers and sisters around the bonfire—honest and moody, yet always looking toward the stars.

And there he is among the blinking light of night, our Star Whisperer—the remnants of his words still lingering in their shimmer: *Let there be light*. When I stand around the fire, I am reminded that each day carries enough of its own problems. My worry and anxiety help nothing. There, under the shimmering, the day melts away and only the transcendence of the night remains. That transcendence is God and his Word—our shield, our hope, and our light.

The fire crackles, the sparks drift upward, and as I relax my mind, my heart opens once again. I am caught, longing for more.

Timothy D. Willard
Oxford, England

Joy

Aching for Heaven

> So if you're serious about living this new resurrection life with Christ, act like it. Pursue the things over which Christ presides. Don't shuffle along, eyes to the ground, absorbed with the things right in front of you. Look up, and be alert to what is going on around Christ—that's where the action is. See things from his perspective.
>
> Colossians 3:1–2 The Message

A friend of mine once told me, "I find myself aching for heaven more these days." What a striking thought.

This morning I woke up far from heaven. You know this kind of morning? When you pass from bed to the shower to the coffee press, numb and overcome? I don't have down days often, but this morning I found myself spinning into a dark place filled with self-pity and anxiety. No thoughts of heaven, only thoughts of Tim.

How do you recalibrate on a morning like this? Money's tight, the joy of work replaced by drudgery, relationships seemingly splintered. How do you gain a foothold in order to climb from the pit?

That was me this morning, shuffling along with my eyes to the ground, absorbed with all the things right in front of me. Then I poured some coffee, closed my eyes, and listened to a favorite song. With my eyelids shut, my vision returned as I considered the apostle Paul's call to look up.

"One, two, three . . . ready or not!" My daughters laughing in the downstairs halls. The sizzle and aroma of the salsa for my breakfast burrito. The growing tummy of my pregnant wife, the mystery of life—from life—and its glow emanating from her face.

Tiny life episodes like these spark daily for each of us, sending time on its way as we each grow along its line. "Look up, and be alert to what is going on around Christ. . . . See things from his perspective."

Today's Prayer

Lord Jesus, am I living in the joy of my work? Am I living in the joy of my family and friends? Or am I too caught up with the hubbub to notice?

Lilies and Birds   DAY 2

You have put more joy in my heart than they have when their grain and wine abound.

Psalm 4:7

I think joy carries a sound, one like the sounds or language of heaven. And hidden within or beyond that sound is the place where I long to be, the "thing" I long to possess. Kierkegaard talks about that sound in the form of a song in his beautiful essay "The Lily in the Field, the Bird of the Air":

What joy when the day dawns and the birds awaken early to the joy of the day; what joy, although tuned to another key, when the evening draws near and the birds hasten joyously home to their nests; and what joy all the long summer day!

What joy when the bird—who does not merely sing at his work like a joyous laborer, but whose essential work it is to sing—joyfully begins its song; what new joy when there upon its neighbor begins, and then its opposite neighbor; and when then the whole chorus joins in, what joy; and when at last it is like a sea of tones to which forest and vale, heaven and earth, respond, a sea of tones in which he who struck the first note now tumbles head over heels with joy—what joy![1]

I'm now a whole day and six hundred words from my dark and splintered spiral of a morning (see yesterday's entry). And I can hear a new song now. It sounds nothing like my pity party, it sounds like heaven—like the joy of birds. Can you hear it?

If you can't, take a moment and look up. What do you see? A ceiling? Clouds? Open blue? Now close your eyes and allow your heart to look up—toward the things of Christ. What are those things right now in your everyday? A co-worker in need of encouragement? A family member who needs prayer? A neighbor who needs help?

Our daily posture toward God reflects in our posture toward those we interact with and care most about in the everyday. In order to hear the joy of birds we must daily assume a life posture of prayer—prayer-like breathing. A simple, short prayer that you repeat throughout the day can become a great weapon as you war through the anxious thoughts and notions that seek to steal your joy.

Today's Prayer

Lord Jesus, you are my joy. You are my joy, and you fill my heart.

Clear My Soul   DAY 3

Today's Prayer

Thanks to Thee, O God, that I have risen to-day,
To the rising of this life itself;
May it be to Thine own glory, O God of every gift,
And to the glory of my soul likewise.

O great God, aid Thou my soul
With the aiding of Thine own mercy;
Even as I clothe my body with wool,
Cover Thou my soul with the shadow of Thy wing.

Help me to avoid every sin,
And the source of every sin to forsake;
And as the mist scatters on the crest of the hills,
May each ill haze clear from my soul, O God.[2]

Beauty Unexpected   DAY 4

For you make him most blessed forever; you make him glad with
the joy of your presence.

Psalm 21:6

Sometimes beauty comes to us unexpectedly in the quiet corners of the day.

The interruption of pouring rain outside your window. Watching a chipmunk scale your blueberry bush, stealing away with the blue treasure. Hearing a song that used to be one of your favorites, from a different time, a different life. Overhearing your daughter discover the moon while the sun still shines.

The unexpected. The interruptions.

And there, in the quiet corner of your day, God finds you. There he wraps you in his whispers: "Blessed are you . . . blessed are you."

You, the blessed one. You, the happy one.

Be on the lookout for unexpected beauty. Be aware of the interruptions accompanied by beauty. It's here we find the joy of birds. It's here we find that God is not only aware of us but actively wooing us. For the interruptions are mere signposts—beautiful placards of joy pointed directly at the One who loves us.

Today's Prayer

Lord Jesus, may your beauty come to me in the moment I need it most. Your compassions are new every morning. Bless me with your interruptions.

Children of the Wind   DAY 5

May the God of hope fill you with all joy and peace in believing, so that by the power of the Holy Spirit you may abound in hope.

Romans 15:13

We cannot conceive of a world where belief in God does not exist. And yet we're often content to live like our belief is not so. What do our contradictory actions do to our belief? Do they perform irreparable damage, ruining the faith we claim?

Perhaps. For faith does not consist of mere intellectual assent. One does not claim faith and explicit belief in God and then go on his merry way. On the contrary, when we face God and believe, we live forever changed, body and soul. We experience a holy renaissance; we are born again and live life as children of God. Faith is not merely a claim, it is a way of life.

In John the Beloved's gospel account, we read that anyone born of the Spirit lives life resembling the wind; a life blowing where it pleases, a life that bears a mysteriously beautiful sound (3:8).

We are children of the Wind!

And yet we live walled up, keeping the buffer of nonchalance between our true identity and us.

When you believe in God, when you believe in what his Son, Christ Jesus, did upon the cross, you become in essence what you believe. You claim Christ and live in him. That's what it means to become a child—you bear the fingerprint, the soul-print, of your parent.

What will this year hold for us, the children of the Wind?

Will we fill the sails of our faith, navigating the tumultuous waters of the unknown? Or will we content ourselves in the safe places of the calm and predictable? Will we allow our culture to dictate our identity? Or will we rise above and transcend like our glorious Father—the Abba of our faith?

Today's Prayer

Lord Jesus, let us remember Paul's words and not forget the past, to press on toward the goal of our faith—Christ himself, our claim and our life!

Grant us the wisdom to discern what it means to press into this heavenly goal within our immediate contexts: how our belief translates to how we love our spouses, raise our children, operate our businesses, and chase our dreams.

Let us not give in to a culture of cynicism and nonchalance, but recapture the romance, glory, and joy of our faith—belief that flies us home, belief that sails us into the beyond.

Love

Are You There?

My soul thirsts for God, for the living God. When can I go and meet with God?

Psalm 42:2 NIV

A re you there, God, around the corner? Is that you in the cello, bowing brilliance into my ears? Did I just miss you in the orange and pink evening fade? Was that you weaving your chord of truth in that late-night conversation?

I rush to somehow hear or hold or see you in the predawn coffee time. I feel you as my hands lie upon my daughters' heads and pray: "Thank you, Father, for all our good things. Help us to serve you with them."

I choke on you as I squeeze the words of worship to you in song—sobs that drive me straight to the ground: "O God, you are my God, earnestly I seek you. . . ."

My flesh, like the earth, yearns for you: your water, your sunshine, your completion, your freedom from thorns.

Are you there, around the corner? In the dark hours, in the light? Are you there? Your hand upholds me—reaching around the corner, pulling me in, and I am comforted.

Today's Prayer

Lord Jesus, help me to see your handiwork in the simple things: music, relationships, a short walk. Settle me so that I may notice how you weave your glory into everything. I want to love you, so that I can love others.

Highflying   DAY 2

> Dear friends, let us love one another, for love comes from God. Everyone who loves has been born of God and knows God. Whoever does not love does not know God, because God is love.
>
> 1 John 4:7–8 NIV

Who is worth your love? Do you take love from others yet withhold love when you know it should be given? The Christian love is a heavenly love, given at great cost, and is able to penetrate our darkest corners within so that we can shine it into others.

In today's Scripture passage, John shows us the connecting line of love: love moves out from God, tracing its origin *in* him—it is his nature. God showed himself to us, in the act of sending his one-of-a-kind Son to die for us. Kierkegaard explains the connecting line of love like this:

> Alas, even the wisest and most ingenious purely human conception of love is yet somewhat highflying and wavering; but Christian love goes from heaven to earth. . . . Christian love is not supposed to vault into heaven, for it comes from heaven

26

and with heaven. It grants the beloved all his imperfections and weaknesses and in all his changes remains with him, loving the person it sees.[1]

You and I love not because we find worthy objects to love. Remember the cross! Remember that we are not worthy. We are jerks, terse and stubborn people. We do not deserve God's love, and yet he provided it for us.

Salvation's beauty comes by way of sacrificial love—a love that gives itself up for the unlovable. And that bloody love gave us life. It should be our joy to mime this kind of love.

Today, you and I have the opportunity to bring life to others by way of our sacrificial love. Are you bringing heaven with you into your relationships? Are you so close to God that his nature, his love, overwhelms you in your thoughts and actions?

Today's Prayer

Lord Jesus, may God himself, the God of peace, sanctify me through and through. Let him ease my stubborn ways and release others of my entitlement mind-set. And may you stretch out your arms and love because you can't help it.

My Ancient Beauty DAY 3

Today's Prayer

Lord Jesus,
Late have I loved you, O Beauty ever ancient, ever new, late have I loved you! You were within me, but I was outside, and it was there that I searched for you. In my unloveliness I plunged into the lovely things which you created.
You were with me, but I was not with you. Created things kept me from you; yet if they had not been in you

they would have not been at all. You called, you shouted, and you broke through my deafness.
You flashed, you shone, and you dispelled my blindness. You breathed your fragrance on me; I drew in breath and now I pant for you. I have tasted you, now I hunger and thirst for more. You touched me, and I burned for your peace.

St. Augustine, *Confessions*[2]

My Night-Erasing Dawn   DAY 4

My splendor is gone and all that I had hoped from the Lord.

Lamentations 3:18 NIV

It's the morning after. Pieces of a relationship lay strewn on the floor. The bitter in your mouth sours your coffee. Yesterday began so well. You were thankful, took a walk down the lane, had fun with friends. But somewhere in the day you lost your way.

Or maybe today has been your *everyday*: bitter herbs for breakfast, the day passing your affliction with blind indifference. Doesn't God see you? Does he see me?

But the wonder of days lies in their repetition. The night comes in its starry abyss and the cold deepens in the twilight rising hour. In a holy cosmic gasp, the sunlight cuts the horizon. Within a breath-span, the light erases the night with the warmth of the new day reaching into the valleys—reaching into you and me.

The steadfast love of the Lord never ceases; his mercies never come to an end.

Lamentations 3:22

The light, again, gleams new. Though my afflictions hover, God's compassions linger. They are new every morning. They are my night-erasing dawn.

The new day does not promise to deliver me from my trial or my failings. It acts as the refresher: another day to decide to love, another day to decide to surrender.

> It is good to wait quietly for the salvation of the Lord.
>
> Lamentations 3:26 NIV

God's love does not rescue us from life's pain. It strengthens us, like the light of day strengthens every plant along the valley floor, to endure. As we endure, we mature. Our character grows. And somewhere in the hushed cold of the twilight we blossom. We open full bloom with the rising sun. The pain of growth produced its fruit.

> For the Lord will not cast off forever, but, though he cause grief, he will have compassion according to the abundance of his steadfast love.
>
> Lamentations 3:31–32

Theologian and pastor Jonathan Edwards encourages us with a vision of Christ as the spiritual sun in our lives. He writes:

> The hearts of true believers are greatly comforted and refreshed with the beams of this. The day that this Sun brings on, when it arises, is a pleasant day to them. As the light of the sun is sweet to the bodily eye, so, and much more, is the light of the spiritual Sun sweet to the spiritual eye of the believer. It is a pleasant thing for the eye to behold the sun, but much more pleasant to a believer to behold Jesus Christ that is fairer than the sons of men.
>
> Psalm 45:2

Today's Prayer

Lord Jesus, help this bitterness pass from me. And may your light—that holy and insuppressible brilliance—warm and encourage my spirit.

Love Notes   DAY 5

Kiss me—full on the mouth! Yes! For your love is better than wine, headier than your aromatic oils. The syllables of your name murmur like a meadow brook. No wonder everyone loves to say your name!

                                        Song of Solomon 1:2–3 THE MESSAGE

On this day lift your hands high, for the Lord of Hosts loves you. This heavenly love echoes in our daily reality. It is in the dance of the trees, the cool of the breeze, the hope of calmer seas. How kind of God, the creator, to throw shards of himself all over the landscape and in our relationships.

"Here," he calls. "Here I am in the blasting morning sun! I am giving it to you today, and tomorrow, and the next day, so that you will be reminded of my loving-kindness."

Isn't that what a lover does? They leave notes all over the place in hopes of striking that chord inside of your heart, inside of mine. We read the lines of the note while a shy smile eases across our face. The sweet delight of hearing from a lover in the unexpected quickens our step.

Love notes. Even the sound of it rings with adolescent nostalgia. The secrecy, and anticipation, the rush of blood to the fast-beating heart. We have to tell someone about this love. We must hide this love deep inside. We must do something with it. We must.

And that is what today is, a giant love note that quickens our step if only we have eyes and ears to see and hear it. The secrecy of the sunset, the anticipation of the stars, the rush of blood as we move from coffee to drive to walk to hellos and good-byes.

Today's Prayer

Lord Jesus, thank you for remembering me with your daily notes of love. Give me eyes to see your tenderness and ears to hear your voice in the breezy beauty of your love.

Newness

A Secular Compulsion

> It is for freedom that Christ has set us free. Stand firm, then, and do not let yourselves be burdened again by a yoke of slavery.
>
> Galatians 5:1 NIV

I struggle with anger. When I was a boy my anger manifested itself in a punch or kick. Though the physically volatile Tim now sleeps in the cave of self-restraint, the adult Tim struggles to keep anger from moving his mouth, if you know what I mean.

Henri Nouwen says that anger is a secular compulsion, one of the two chief enemies of the spiritual life. He defines anger as the "impulsive response to the experience of being deprived."[1]

Why should I care about what others deny me? I care because I've bought the lie of the world that says my sense of self depends on what I can acquire, be it praise from others or my own way.

When we live more dependent on what culture thinks or says of us, we live as the secular man or woman. But that is not who we are in Christ.

I am a man because I've put on Christ. I am a son of God because I have come to the Father. I am the branch because I have abided in the Vine. I am free from the slavery of sin—that is who I am. That is who you are.

Throw off, dear friend, the bonds of anger or resentment or bitterness—those cousins of anger. Your self-worth does not depend on what you can gain from the world. Your self-worth depends on what you give up and what you gain in Christ. He alone is our peace.

Today's Prayer

Lord Jesus, may your blessings fill my heart, lifting it so that I may sing the song of your love.

Walk in Love   DAY 2

For you were once darkness, but now you are light in the Lord.

Ephesians 5:8 NIV

Therefore, therefore. Paul uses this word in quick succession in his letter to the Ephesians.

Therefore, having put away falsehood, let each one of you speak the truth with his neighbor, for we are members one of another.

Ephesians 4:25

Therefore be imitators of God, as beloved children.

Ephesians 5:1

Therefore prompts us to look back and see what he's saying, and then to look forward, at his exhortation.

Here Paul instructs us to be renewed in our minds, not darkened as the world is. "Therefore" we are to put away falsehood, speaking truth to each other. "Therefore" let the bitterness and anger and disgraceful language fall away. Rather, encourage each other. Let kindness and forgiveness salt your lives.

"Therefore," he says in 5:1, "be imitators of God, as beloved children." Both my daughters love to sit on my little black chair in my study and act like they're studying my books. It's cute, until I find highlighting all over the pages. They imitate me, their father. They giggle, finding pure joy in doing what Daddy does.

Today, look behind you. Look where God has taken you—the mountains and valleys, the dark times and light. Look ahead to the person you've become in him and the one you're constantly becoming. And on this day, think of yourself not in your work, but on your Father's chair, imitating him, in kindness and love and forgiveness and grace.

Today's Prayer

Lord Jesus, I seek to walk in love, as you loved me and gave yourself up for me, a fragrant offering and sacrifice to God (Ephesians 5:2).

Chisel, Wheel, Lightest Word   DAY 3

Today's Prayer

Lord Jesus, today my prayer embeds itself in these words: "Let patience have her perfect work. Statue under the chisel of the sculptor, stand ready to the blows of his mallet. Clay on the wheels, let the fingers of the divine potter mold you at their will. Obey the father's lightest word: hear the brother who knows you and died for you."[2]

Your Shimmering Clothes   DAY 4

And he who was seated on the throne said, "Behold, I am making all things new."

Revelation 21:5

I remember my Sunday school teacher telling us about the Road to Damascus.

Picture the brilliance of the Damascus encounter: the blinding light of the Christ ironically erasing Paul's physical sight for a time, yet giving him spiritual clarity and understanding into the truth of Jesus and his resurrection.

Paul knows what it means to live alienated from God. Perhaps he reaches back to Damascus in his letter to the Ephesians, as he wields stark imagery to paint a haunting picture of spiritual dichotomy.

In chapter 4, verses 17 to 24, Paul, the former Christian killer, reminds us that the way of the world crumbles in corruption, recognizable by sensual fleshly living.

The passage describes the Gentile way of life. Their darkened hearts and minds reflected in their outward life. Their vain thinking and ignorance resulted in the hardening of their hearts. As such, they fell prey to all kinds of sensuality, greed, and lusts.

Then the passage shifts. The transition introduces *the way of Christ*.

Paul calls the reader toward the truth found in Christ. He exhorts: Disregard your former way of life marked by the corruption of the inner self—"deceitful desires"—in favor of a *new way* punctuated by a *new self.*

How do we become new? We renew the spirit of the mind. We are to "put on" the new self. Inward renewal comes from clothing ourselves with divine attributes: true righteousness and holiness.

Today's Prayer

Lord Jesus, inside of me the shadows persist. But your light envelops darkness. Cleanse my thoughts today of the shadows. I want to bask in the newness that is you, covering me.

Release Your Heart to Christ   DAY 5

Put off your old self, which belongs to your former manner of life . . . and put on the new self.

Ephesians 4:22, 24

Where the life of the flesh fails due to ignorance and an inward hardening, the life of the Spirit soars. It is as if Paul opens an imaginary door to expose the path of the world, and then turns us around to show us a way totally other: Christ's way to live, Christ's way to be.

But the beauty of this "putting on" comes in this: It's not *just* a new self we put on. It is a new man, a new woman.

Who is the new person we put on?

This putting on of the new person "is not so much a question of personal *imatio Christi* as of incorporation into Christ," says theologian F. F. Bruce. "The new man or new humanity is Christ himself," he continues, "not Christ in isolation from his people but Christ *in* his people."[3]

How do we stop living like the world? We put on Christ! And how do we put on Christ himself? We allow our hearts—our darkened and ignorant hearts—to be renewed by him.

Today's Prayer

Lord Jesus, teach us what it means to put you on. Strengthen our kindness. Quiet our profane tongues. Cut through our pretenses. We don't want to grieve you through selfish and sensual living. We want your renewal. We want you.

Thirst

Groping for God

> From one man he made every nation of the human race to in-
> habit the entire earth, determining their set times and the fixed
> limits of the places where they would live, so that they would
> search for God and perhaps grope around for him and find him,
> though he is not far from each one of us.
>
> Acts 17:26–27 NET

The forest hung around our necks while the trail meandered off-camber along the mountainside. It was a sketchy dusk hike—light enough to see yet dark enough to fall. We emerged from the winding tree tunnel onto a river rock field. It was mid-summer in Vermont's Green Mountains, so the river was low, just patches of moon-colored water here and there.

We built a fire on a small archipelago, played guitar, and chatted as night fell. Our return hike found the mountainside tunnel pitch-black. We made a torch out of an old T-shirt and a stick. It illuminated the path briefly. The rest of the one-mile jaunt was in darkness.

We groped our way along the mountainside tunnel, banging our shins and feeling our way. We emerged at the trailhead strained but happy to be out of the tunnel.

I remember the stress felt by some within our band of eight hikers. I remember the frustration that accompanied the lack of familiarity with the path. I remember reaching out to find nothing.

Groping in the night is different from searching in light. In order to find my way to the riverbed and back again I had to reach out into darkness, wave my hands in front of me, and search for directional clues. I had to continue on at a certain cautious pace. It was nerve-racking and demanded singular concentration.

I wonder how many of us grope for God.

In the Old Testament we find verses like Jeremiah 29:13 ("You will seek me and find me, when you seek me with all your heart") and others[1] that make it clear: God wants us to seek him, and hard.

In the New Testament, Paul, in Acts 17, challenges the Athenians' worldview as he addresses the general council at the Areopagus. In his speech Paul says God made the earth and mankind the way he did so that man would "grope" around and perhaps find him even though he's not really that far away (vs. 24–27).

Paul uses a graphic term from which we get "groping"—like feeling your way around in the darkness—*straining* to find him.

I wonder how many of us today will grope for God. I wonder how many of us strain for God with the full strength of our wills and minds. Old Testament writers weren't promoting an emotionalism but rather a deliberate and daily grope that required volitional determination and intelligence. To be sure, emotion plays a part, but only insofar as it prompts you to search with all your strength.

Today's Prayer

Lord Jesus, I am reaching for you today, straining for all your goodness with every ounce of my will and every fiber of my intellect. Help me throw off all that keeps me distracted from knowing you more.

Our Blessed Pursuit   DAY 2

Yes, I'm on my way! I'll be there soon!

Revelation 22:12 THE MESSAGE

Do not lose hope today. Yes, God may *seem* far, but he is in fact quite close. Only, weigh your pursuits. What is top of mind for you today? Is he included? Or what has replaced him? What strains your grace? Is it anxiety over bills, or perhaps the lack of feeling in your life? You don't feel him, and so you suspect he is far off.

Maybe he is far off at the moment, if only because everything else in your life has pushed him far. On this day of days, press hard into prayer and consider the encouraging words of A. W. Tozer:

> What I am anxious to see in Christian believers is a beautiful paradox. I want to see in them the joy of finding God while at the same time they are blessedly pursuing Him. I want to see in them the great joy of having God yet always wanting Him.[2]

Today's Prayer

Lord Jesus, all this stuff invading my brain and my heart has pushed you from my senses. I know this is because I lack trust. Help me when I am weak today. Revive my affections so that I can, once again, pursue you with the vigor I so desperately seek.

Satisfying Myself   DAY 3

Today, dear reader, consider to what extent you have been living for yourself. You and I cannot expect to find spiritual depth or satisfaction when we walk out on God and fulfill the desires of our flesh. In preparation for tomorrow's reflection, read Jeremiah chapter two. But today, may our prayer be one of confession to the Lord.

Today's Prayer

Lord Jesus, I have committed a compound sin: I've walked out on you, the fountain—my fountain—of fresh flowing waters, and then dug cisterns—cisterns that leak, cisterns that are no better than sieves. I have found the life-giving waters of Christ, and, out of fear of the Holy One, I have fallen back. I'm afraid to drink because my sins have heaped up all around me. I have found myself entangled.

Are You Not Thirsty?   DAY 4

For my people have committed two evils; they have forsaken me the fountain of living waters, and hewed them out cisterns, broken cisterns, that can hold no water.

Jeremiah 2:13 KJV

I love the scene in C. S. Lewis's *The Silver Chair* where Aslan invites Jill to drink from the stream. But, like you and I often do, Jill wants to drink from another stream—one farther away from Aslan. Jesus beckons you and me to come taste and see. But we turn toward the mirror of success, the mirror of power, the mirror of self for refreshment, all the while dying of thirst.

"Are you not thirsty?" said the Lion.

"I'm *dying* of thirst," said Jill.

"Then drink," said the Lion.

"May I—could I—would you mind going away while I do?" said Jill.

Later, Jill frantically says, "I daren't come and drink."

"Then you will die of thirst," said the Lion.

"Oh dear!" said Jill, coming another step nearer. "I suppose I must go and look for another stream then."

"There is no other stream," said the Lion.[3]

I fear, at times, we, like Jill, fear what the Lion will do to us if we drink, and so we drift off into the woods and look for our own stream. We look for "the good" in other things, thinking this and that are the streams we need. And, in our error, we shrivel, slowly dying of thirst.

The road to our true selves is really a road to the one stream. In the story, Jill does drink—she sips the revelation of refreshment. It's cold and fully satisfies.

Today's Prayer

Lord Jesus, I want always to drink the cold, satisfying waters of your love, your reality, and your goodness. Guide me to your stream, Christ my love.

As the Deer   DAY 5

As a deer pants for flowing streams, so pants my soul for you, O God.

Psalm 42:1

I'm so tired. I want to give in. When we're weary in body, we waver in our spirit. Our desires fall into the mud and the carnal "us" takes over. The extra drink we know we shouldn't have. The bit of food that we know we should resist. The trashy program we know hinders our minds and imaginations.

With so much at our fingertips, via the Internet, television, movies, gaming systems, food, drink, and so on, it's easy to convince ourselves we deserve an extra bit as a reward for our hard day.

But it's at this point when something good can bend toward the ugly.

Thomas à Kempis, the great Christian mystic, reminds us in his classic work *The Imitation of Christ* that if a person satisfies "his desires, remorse of conscience overwhelms him because he followed his passions and they did not lead to the peace he sought.

"True peace of heart, then, is found in resisting passions, not in satisfying them. There is no peace in the carnal man, in the man given to vain attractions, but there is peace in the fervent and spiritual man."[4]

But Thomas's words here do not direct us to legalism. Rather, they steer us toward him for whom we should pant: Jesus Christ. David's words in the psalm above haunt us in a world of machines and screens. We are not familiar with animal desire. How intense a thirst it must be for a deer to pant—for the deer runs and bounds, never seeming to tire. And yet it not only thirsts, it pants. It is tired. It has run long, up mountains, across streams, over rocks, through the thicket in search of refreshment.

To what do we turn when our days fill with mountain climbing, stream crossings, thicket navigating? Do we merely satisfy the immediate desire of our flesh? Or are we panting for something more?

Today's Prayer

Lord Jesus, I only want you. More and more I seek your constant filling. You alone are my desire. Fill me today. Satisfy, even more this moment, my enduring thirst.

Hope

Our Dripping Song of Hope

> Worship the Lord in the splendor of holiness; tremble before him, all the earth!
>
> Psalm 96:9

In Psalm 96 the psalter uses the word *beauty*. It's one of the few places in the English Bible the word is used, and it's used to describe God. The poet emphasizes his description by using parallel couplets: *splendor and majesty // strength and beauty* (v. 6). God's glory is emphasized throughout this psalm. His glory begins in general and even vast terms at the beginning of the psalm, then funnels down into the specifics of fields and trees and seas.

The action words catch the reader and propel her into a rhythm: "sing . . . declare . . . ascribe . . . worship . . . say." They are instructions for the worshiper, imploring, even demanding that they worship God with this, their new song. And what is this new song?

It is overflow of the heart—a heart opened and humbled by God's majesty. The only thing the worshiper is able to do is sing, because only the poetry of a song can capture the splendor of the Maker. At best we can only paint pictures with our words, words that dance into our songs.

What is this song for the individual worshiper? A beautiful thought that you and I each have a song to offer! And what of the last stanza?

> Let the heavens be glad, and let the earth rejoice;
>   let the sea roar, and all that fills it;
> let the field exult, and everything in it!
> Then shall all the trees of the forest sing for joy
> before the Lord, for he comes,
>   for he comes to judge the earth.
> He will judge the world in righteousness,
>   and the peoples in his faithfulness.
>   Psalm 96:11–13

Here we find the hope of our theology: a loving and faithful, majestic and righteous judge. He comes to judge the world in righteousness, his people in his faithfulness. What does this say about God himself? We see clearly the judging aspect of God and the context of that judgment.

And in this righteous Judge do we place our hope. In him our faith comes alive and we sing our new song—a song dripping with the tones of hope, with the wonder of poetry . . . all that our language can muster we use to explain the worth of our heavenly Judge.

Interesting that glory and beauty are found in his strength. The beauty of our sanctuary turns out to be the Strong One himself—he is the one the sea creatures praise and the leaves and trees exalt with their clapping. All creation resounds with the praise of God.

If you read this song over and over and listen, you can hear the echoes of his hope and righteousness moving through the trees, you can feel the massive glory, what we call beauty, covering us all.

When there is nothing to say.

When we can't stand or rest.

When we have no words, we have Psalm 96.

Today's Prayer

Lord Jesus, I am seeking hope this morning. I wait for your song of beauty this evening. I have no words, only the groan of praise for you. I lift you up.

Finding Your New Song   DAY 2

> I waited patiently for the Lord to help me,
> and he turned to me and heard my cry.
> He lifted me out of the pit of despair,
> out of the mud and the mire.
> He set my feet on solid ground
> and steadied me as I walked along.
> He has given me a new song to sing,
> a hymn of praise to our God.
> Many will see what he has done and be amazed.
> They will put their trust in the Lord.
>
> Psalm 40:1–3 NLT

Yesterday started out with epiphanies and ended with wonder. Today, not so much. Relate?

I found myself exhausted by midafternoon and almost falling asleep as I waited for my daughters to finish their cereal before bed. And so life moves on. Today the mountaintop, tomorrow the valley.

Where are you today, tonight?

We escape the pit of despair by waiting, enduring. Patience implies trust, and with trust comes blessing. The blessing? Steady ground—maybe not a day of epiphanies and wonder, but a day where we find the confidence to sing a new song.

Find your new song this week. Wait on him. Trust and you will find the solid ground

Today's Prayer

Lord Jesus, to him who is able to keep me from stumbling and to present me before his glorious presence without fault and with great joy—amen. In the quiet I seek the newness you give.

Taste and See   DAY 3

Today's Prayer

Lord Jesus, I cannot always see you, even in your invisible ways. Some days even the sky feels like the top of a cage. What is hope that I should run to it? And you answer, "Hope looks like your hand reaching for that which your heart loves. You cannot have hope and not love. Hope reaches into the invisible, sure of its prize. And love does not disappoint.

"For I am love, and it is me your hope reaches to seize. Do you despair when you cannot see? Do you falter when beauty seems scarce? Even youths grow tired and weak; and so, my Love, revive yourself. Rest your reaching heart, and taste and see. I bring rest on the wings of hope."

You are ever my hope. I fall into you, caught in the unending glory of your love.

How Hope Ignites   DAY 4

We always pray for you, and we give thanks to God, the Father of our Lord Jesus Christ. For we have heard of your faith in Christ Jesus and your love for all of God's people, which come from your confident hope of what God has reserved for you in heaven. You have had this expectation ever since you first heard the truth of the Good News.

Colossians 1:3–5 NLT

Hope fuels our faith and our love. Or at least it should. It did so for the Christians in Colossae. Paul loved hearing about their faithful, loving testimony. This kind of living was fueled by an anticipatory lifestyle—of a people looking toward heaven. That was their hope, the hope of future glory.

I was touring the country in a van when I fell in love with my wife. I was playing music and she was finishing graduate school. We longed to be together. What's more, we longed for the day when we'd consummate our relationship on our wedding night.

We lived in anticipation, and that longing fueled our love and painted each day with beauty and hope.

What does it look like to live in anticipation of the coming glory of Christ? How would such a longing affect our lifestyle, our choices, our consumption, and our priorities?

Is eternity simmering in your heart?

Today's Prayer
Lord Jesus, simmer in me. You are eternity—the place I long to be. You are my evermore, my soul-lover, my body-creator. My hope is not only in you, it is you.

Highest Dignity   DAY 5

Now he has reconciled you by Christ's physical body through death to present you holy in his sight, without blemish and free from accusation—if you continue in your faith, established and firm, and do not move from the hope held out in the gospel.

Colossians 3:22–23 NIV

I n Paul's letter to the Colossae Christians, he reminds them to keep Christ central in all they do: " . . . that in everything he might be preeminent" (1:18). For Christ to remain preeminent in our lives, it means that he is chief over everything. It means he holds the first rank of highest dignity.

This verse resounds in my heart because too often I leave Christ out of my decisions and my everyday living. Pride chokes out the Light of Christ far too often. And yet daily I press into Christ and ask for the courage to obey, for strength to decrease so that he can increase. And when I find myself in that beautiful place where Christ holds the first rank of highest dignity, I pine for heaven and all the glory of God therewith.

In Revelation 4–5, John steps into heaven and observes a worship service unlike any other. Try reading these chapters in one sitting. The writing is glorious and will ignite a hope of heaven and awaken the eternity within you. It will draw you toward Christ, the Slain Lamb of God. You will throw up your hands in praise as you sense the Holy Spirit strengthen your faith and galvanize your love.

Today's Prayer

Lord Jesus, I find peace in your Word. "Weep no more," you say, for "behold, the Lion of the tribe of Judah, the Root of David, has conquered. . . ." You are my hope, O Lion, O Christ (Revelation 5:5).

Confession

Living Aware

> When you become aware of your guilt in any of these ways, you must confess your sins.
>
> Leviticus 5:5 NLT

Brothers and sisters, what power does confession hold? It holds the power to bind us close to one another. It holds the power to renew our relationship with the Lord Jesus.

John the Beloved reminds us to confess our sins, because the act of confession can refresh our fellowship with God and one another.

Too often we think confession entails unloading some big sin. Although confession might entail such an unloading, it actually begins simply. It begins with the awareness to see how we have caused a rift or mistreated or in some way wronged a brother or sister or the Lord.

Today's Prayer

Lord Jesus, today I start simply: aware of you, aware of me and my need. I need you as I confess to my friend, to my father, my mother, my sibling, my co-worker. If I confess, you are faithful and just. You will forgive. I pray for such reconciliation in all my relationships.

We Fear Confession   DAY 2

When I refused to confess my sin, my body wasted away, and I groaned all day long. . . . My strength evaporated like water in the summer heat.

Psalm 32:3–4 NLT

Why is it so hard to confess to one another? Because our pride tells us we have nothing to confess, or that whatever we have to confess will be too embarrassing, or that we will lose control of a position of power. Pride dupes us into living a lie. Such is not life, but a heavy existence of guilt.

The act of confession draws us toward one another. But we fail to take that first step toward fellowship. All it takes is seven words: I was wrong, will you forgive me?

A confession!

Think about how sweet your friendships would be if confession and forgiveness were our common language. Imagine how our marriages might shine if confession and forgiveness replaced pride and selfishness.

Today's Prayer

Lord Jesus, help me confess my sins to you and to people whom I love. Strengthen me to pray for them so that we find healing.

Pull Me Close   DAY 3

Today's Prayer

*Lord Jesus, here I sit in the sanctuary of your grace.
When I close my eyes and think of my need, confession rises into my eyes and tears fall. You move me to
confession—to that beautiful place of wholeness. Pull
me close to you, Lord Jesus, as I seek to pull close to
those whom I love as well. Your kindness to me compels
my humility; it prompts my confession. How wonderful
when pride falls at my feet and I utter those words, "I was
wrong, will you forgive me?" I praise you, Lord Jesus;
your completeness guides me into the constant flow of
your forgiveness, strengthening my heart so that confession is ever on my lips.*

Praise, Confess, Ask   DAY 4

Therefore confess your sins to each other and pray for each other
so that you may be healed. The prayer of a righteous person is
powerful and effective.

James 5:16 NIV

Our lack of confession within our lives boils down to our
inability to communicate. We live in an age where the machine now sits in our hands: We read emails, blogs, and news;
we text, call, email. And yet with such a powerful device we
seem inept at cultivating true relationships. We must do more
than send messages back and forth. We must plunge deep into
the real of each other's lives.

The same ineptitude also plagues our heavenly relationship. Consider the words of theologian and minister Richard Baxter:

> Little do we know how we wrong ourselves by shutting out of our prayers the praises of God, or allowing them so narrow a room as we usually do, while we are copious enough in our confessions and petitions. Reader, I entreat thee, remember this: let praises have a larger room in thy duties; keep matter ready at hand to feed thy praise, as well as matter for confession and petition. To this end study the excellencies and goodness of the Lord as frequently as thy own wants and unworthiness; the mercies thou has received, and those which are promised, as often as the sins thou hast committed.[1]

Baxter's words remind us that in true communion with one another and with our Lord, we must be always praising, always confessing, always asking. Communion, then, entails honesty and transparency, a willingness to engage.

Today's Prayer

Lord Jesus, I want to speak to you with real words that describe my real feelings. Keep the veneer of relationships far from me. Strengthen my boldness so I may confess. Enliven my heart so I may praise. Free my heart so I may ask as a child asks of her father.

Into Worship   DAY 5

If we confess our sins, he is faithful and just and will forgive us our sins and purify us from all unrighteousness.

1 John 1:9 NIV

For several years we attended a church that offered communion each week after the sermon. This was a change for my wife and me, but we quickly found the practice to be an important part of our week.

Not to overgeneralize, but men are not always the best at asking forgiveness. Admitting we are wrong, well, that is even more rare. During the communion time at church, however, I saw a window of opportunity to step out of my comfort zone and do some real work in my marriage relationship.

Before my wife and I would approach the communion table, we prayed together, and it was during this intimate time of prayer that I found the opportunity to confess. The words were simple and whispered: "Lord, forgive me for my harsh tone with my wife. I confess to you the sins of a broken and rebellious heart." Then I would reference a specific occurrence in which I was obtuse or not loving.

This brief and vulnerable time reestablished our love and helped to pass our differences into God's love—a heavenly love that covers. From confessing to my wife, I learned how to better confess to my Lord. Now, daily, I find myself confessing unaware.

We should confess to one another and to the Lord, not just because it's an imperative from God, but because of the beauty it invites into our relationships.

Today's Prayer
Lord Jesus, I confess . . . [You can finish the rest].

Courage

The Great Desert Runner   DAY 1

Praise be to the Lord, to God our Savior, who daily bears our burdens.

Psalm 68:19 NIV

Our memories can be powerful instruments in our spiritual shaping. In Psalm 68, David invokes Israel's history. God rescued Israel from Egyptian slavery. God, the Great Desert Runner, led his wilderness people out of their oppression. With fierce kindness God leads his people to victory.

But there is more to this processional psalm than a simple stroll down memory lane. We also see David reflecting on his own experience of leading the ark of the covenant to Mount Zion. Remember that scene? When the procession reaches the city, David famously dances before the Lord—his adoration for God expressed making himself undignified.

Through the power of God's love we are able to look upon our past with gratitude and unhinged praise to the One who leads us from the desert lands of captivity to the glories of his throne.

Our God is a God who saves; from the Sovereign Lord comes
escape from death.

Psalm 68:20 NIV

When David reaches back into the past of his people, no doubt
he sees his own past—his journey from the open lands beneath
the stars caring for sheep, to killing the bear and the lion, to the
inside of the king's chamber, to the battlegrounds themselves.
He sees that Israel's history is his own history. He responds to the
memory with praise, and that praise is the hyssop for his "today."

Your today is never so dismal that God cannot lavish his
freeing power upon you. Are you wasting away in the wilderness of today? Remember that the Great Desert Runner comes
for you; he *always* comes for you. And he will lead you from
the wilderness with the graceful leading only he can provide.

Today's Prayer

*Lord Jesus, we exalt you! Summon your power, O God;
show us your strength, O God, as you have done before.
So let it be.*

Dance, Clap Hands, Leap, Roll On DAY 2

And the special gift of ministry you received when I laid hands
on you and prayed—keep that ablaze! God doesn't want us to
be shy with his gifts, but bold and loving and sensible.

2 Timothy 1:5–7 THE MESSAGE

Children don't know any better. They sing, they dance, they
run with near reckless abandon. When did you cease to be
childlike? Did the world sink its talons into you and steal away
your innocence?

With age and maturation come the wrinkles of shame and timidity. Life hurts us, and we'll not be so naïve as to let it happen again. Add to that the pressure of this world to look and act a certain way, and the idea of childlike faith—of working *with* the Holy Spirit to do something uncommon, of living a faith unguarded and free—seems a luxury we can no longer afford.

In today's Scripture passage we find Paul encouraging his young protégé, Timothy. Paul reminds him of the Spirit alive within him. The strength of our faith is, paradoxically, the childlikeness of it.

> O to have my life henceforth a poem of new joys!
> To dance, clap hands, exult, shout, skip, leap, roll on,
>   float on . . .
> "Poem of Joys," Walt Whitman,
> *Leaves of Grass*

Do not misinterpret childlike faith as an innocent naïveté. When Paul reminds Timothy to be bold, he is exhorting him to use his giftedness with confidence. Do not toss out shyness as an excuse to remain stagnant in your spiritual life. Be bold with it, says Paul. Active use of your giftedness will produce spiritual boldness. You will pray more fervently. You will step out in faith more often. You will develop spiritual courage while at the same time maintaining the childlike whimsy of your faith—one that shouts, skips, leaps, and rolls on for Christ.

Today's Prayer

Lord Jesus, I am often shy about my giftedness. I am not trying to put forth a false humility, but I fear what others might think. I fear failure. I fear. I fear. But you cast out fear—for you are love and your love emblazons my faith. Help me to run and skip and roll on.

Today It Does Not Have to Be   DAY 3

Today's Prayer

Lord Jesus, today you tell, you tell me it does not have to be—this abuse, this strangeness, this aloneness, this dark. You tell me, O Friend of Slaves, to rise. Reach past compromise. Take up arms against the woe of the world. I will not break today, for you, my Rock, have mended me, placed me upon high ground, and set me free. You have given me a holy task—that of living. Each breath, each word, each blink of the eye does not hide from you, O Creator of bodies and Giver of breath.

And so today does not have to be yesterday. Rather, today springs new, like daffodils that shoot up, wave in the wind, and bloom into yellows and whites. Each spring they rise. And today is my "each spring." I rise with you. I rise for you. For you, O Sweet One, rose for me.

Be Strong and Very Courageous   DAY 4

Be strong and courageous. Do not be afraid or terrified because of them, for the Lord your God goes with you; he will never leave you nor forsake you.

Deuteronomy 31:6 NIV

Remember, dear reader, courage-talk is not just a pep talk. Pep talks work well in sports, but we do not play at life. We live it. God's words to Joshua remain ever popular because so many of us need encouragment. We need courage.

Keep in mind that God is not offering Joshua and the Israelites a shot in the arm, a "go get 'em!" speech. He's digging into their weakness and challenging them. Keep your faith strong and be steadfast in your courage, he says—the very thing they struggled with earlier (see Deuteronomy 1:26–36).

Is God wagging his holy finger at them, almost teasing them? No, quite the contrary. His message sounds similar to the message he gives to us through Christ Jesus: "I have already gone before you. I have promised that I will come through for you, and I will. You can take courage, my son, my daughter, because I will never leave you nor forsake you." In Deuteronomy 31:23 God says, "Be strong and courageous, for you will bring the Israelites into the land I promised them on oath, *and I myself will be with you*" (NIV).

Today's Prayer

Lord Jesus, I know in the past I have wavered. I continue to say the right things about faith and being steadfast, but I falter. Forgive my weak faith and strengthen me, O my God! Be my strength—for you will never leave me. You are the strong one. You are the steadfast one. As I put you on—my spiritual clothing—may your courage be mine.

No Mere Indifference DAY 5

For everything in the world—the lust of the flesh, the lust of the eyes, and the pride of life—comes not from the Father but from the world.

1 John 2:16 NIV

A line in Søren Kierkegaard's *The Sickness Unto Death* haunts me: "For worldliness is precisely to ascribe infinite value to the indifferent." Kierkegaard believed the world only cares about itself; it limits its knowledge and love for things beautiful to what is immediate. It busies itself with itself—the indifferent, the unconcerned, the wise ways of the world. When we adopt this view of the world, we too become indifferent, nonchalant, and callous.

This line of thought forces me to ask myself: Have I become indifferent to life? Is there a kind of despair that seeks to cheat me out of my very own self?

It is day five today. Perhaps, like me, you're staring at a weekend of busyness. It is busy because it has duped you, like it has duped me. I've bought in to the ways of the world, as Kierkegaard says:

> Yes, what we call worldliness simply consists of such people who, if one may so express it, pawn themselves to the world. They use their abilities, amass wealth, carry out worldly enterprises, make prudent calculations, etc., and perhaps are mentioned in history, but they are not themselves. In a spiritual sense they have no self, no self for whose sake they could venture everything, no self for God—however selfish or otherwise.[1]

We know from our reflection yesterday that we do not procure courage from a pep talk. Rather, courage lives in our actions and reactions. How will I respond to the bully at school or the passive-aggressive boss at work? I will respond with courage, relying on God to carry me, to guide me, to never leave me.

So as we each stare into a despairing world that seeks to derail our courage and cheat us of our true selves, we need the courage that comes from heaven.

Today's Prayer

Lord Jesus, the world wants to cheat me of your great wonder. It seeks to blindside me with wealth, status, and power. My flesh desires those things, but my soul thirsts for you. Keep me locked into you, not indifferent or shadowed by nonchalance. I want to burn from within, for you.

Work

Voice Crying Out

Thunder in the desert! "Prepare for God's arrival!
Make the road straight and smooth, a highway fit for our God.
Fill in the valleys, level off the hills,
Smooth out the ruts, clear out the rocks.
Then God's bright glory will shine and everyone will see it. Yes.
Just as God has said."

Isaiah 40:3–5 THE MESSAGE

Each time someone asks John the Baptist about his identity or about his role or about Jesus, he uses it to point to the importance of Jesus. Remember, Jesus and John were baptizing people at the same time. But John was quick to offer the distinction between himself and Jesus.

"I am like one crying out in the wilderness," he says, using the words of Isaiah the prophet.

"Are you Elijah?"

"No."

"Are you a prophet?

"No. I am nothing but a faraway voice. Listen to Jesus."

John knows his role in life. Though he is confident and bold, he is careful not to allow a blind spot to catch him unawares. When he says the famous line, "He must increase, and I must decrease," he is not slouching away. He had accomplished much, but now it was time for Christ and his ministry. John held his accomplishments in open hands. "Okay, God, I'm thankful for the opportunity to serve and to preach, now it's your Son's turn."

Blind spots creep in when we live life unaware. We can become so wrapped up in ourselves—our own work, our own voice, and our own success—that we isolate ourselves from Jesus.

Today's Prayer

Lord Jesus, help me today to be aware of my blind spots. What grief, pain, or anxiety am I causing that I'm not aware of? Does my treatment of the ones I love darken because of the deep muck of pride I cannot seem to wade through? I want others to see you today. I want my voice to be secondary—a faraway voice—so that your voice can speak through me.

Good Work   DAY 2

Make it your ambition to lead a quiet life: You should mind your own business and work with your hands. . . .

1 Thessalonians 4:11 NIV

How often do we consider our work—what it is, how we perform it, or why we are doing it? Think about your work, be it a home-educator to little ones, or marketing director, student, or poet. Do you abide by the words of God in your work—what he wants from you, what he wants you to give to others through your work?

"Good human work honors God's work," writes the poet Wendell Berry. "Good work uses no thing without respect, both for what it is in itself and for its origin. It uses neither tool nor material that it does not respect and that it does not love. It honors nature as a great mystery and power, as an indispensable teacher, and as the inescapable judge of all work of human hands. It does not disassociate life and work, or pleasure and work, or love and work, or usefulness and beauty.

"To work without pleasure or affection, to make a product that is not both useful and beautiful, is to dishonor God, nature, the thing that is made, and whomever it is made for. This is blasphemy: to make shoddy work of the work of God. But such blasphemy is not possible when the entire Creation is understood as holy and when the works of God are understood as embodying and thus revealing His spirit."[1]

Do you agree with Berry? What challenges you about his take on work?

Today's Prayer

Lord Jesus, how do I lead a quiet life when the world rages in noise and clamor all day long? How do I stay calm, putting my nose to the grindstone each day when I am so tired? Help me to keep work sacred—as worship to you.

Stepping Into Glory
DAY 3

Today's Prayer

Lord Jesus, how do I keep my work safe within the purpose of your intent? Too often my work mixes with anxiety, both pushed by the greed of society. I lust after things, not even realizing how desperately I covet. When I stray from your purpose I lose sight of my work and it becomes cold, more a means to an end than a chance to give you glory.

Remind me, Lord, how you possess me—how your love leads me toward glory and how my work gives me an opportunity to step into that glory.

His Possession, His Purpose   DAY 4

> But you are a chosen people, a royal priesthood, a holy nation, God's special possession, that you may proclaim the praises of him who called you out of darkness into his wonderful light.
>
> 1 Peter 2:9 NIV

Don't get tripped up over *chosen*. This word refers to our corporate calling as the family of God. It is the idea that God drew close to us. Notice how *God chose* us. He acted first. This action not only shows us his deep love for us as individuals, it helps us understand the origin of our identity. It's in *him*.

How comforting to know God took the first step and desires us—he wants us to realize that our identity originates in his action toward us.

Notice too how we are *God's possession*. I love knowing that God Almighty possesses me. This truth comforts me, it encourages me, it fuels my ideas and creative agency. I feel a sense of pre-accomplishment, like I can do anything because, regardless of the outcome, God possesses me. What peace!

Peter also mentions *how* God set us apart to be a holy nation. This feels similar to possession. As his possession, he sets us aside and makes us special—special in the sense of purpose, his purpose.

Not only does he make us holy, but he views us as his royal priesthood. No mediator necessary! When we want to pray or worship God, we do it. When a friend needs prayer, we pray—we intercede for one another. We encourage and support one another through prayer.

When we approach our work in the peace that comes from knowing that God possesses us, we cease to strive. Not only do we stop striving, we begin serving, interceding. He sets his purpose ablaze in our hearts.

Today's Prayer

Lord Jesus, thank you for possessing me. What joy fills my heart knowing that as I work, I do so for your glory and for your purpose.

Glory Givers   DAY 5

Whatever you do, work heartily, as for the Lord and not for men.

Colossians 3:23

Realize, not only does God possess you and not only did he draw toward you first, but he also called you out of darkness. You may be sitting in your office, your living room, or a café today wondering, *Why am I in this position? How did I get here, at this particular point in my life—and for what?*

You are where you are today because God called you out of darkness. Don't get bogged down with career and "where do I live?" questions. Know that you sit where you sit because God made it so, and he made it so out of love and grace for you as his child.

The question I always ask when writing or speaking to folks is, *So what?* What is the ultimate goal of me being where I am? The apostle Peter says God did all this "that you may declare the praises of him who called you" (1 Peter 2:9 NIV). Translation? Glory!

You are sitting here today for the sole purpose of giving God glory. If knowing you're possessed by God comforts you, how much more freeing is it to think that everything you do as a leader should focus on bringing God glory? Every word, every action, and every thought should spiral into the glory funnel. You and I are here, doing what we do so that we can glorify God. This is why we work.

Today's Prayer

Lord Jesus, you release me from people's expectations by giving me purpose, and that is for your glory. Thank you for firing my soul with glory.

Silence

The Company of Crowds

> In quietness and in trust shall be your strength.
>
> Isaiah 30:15

The spiritual disciplines usually receive one of four responses from Christians. They are either ignored completely, wished for but not pursued, become the trinkets of trend, or they become life-giving characteristics deeply experienced in the presence of Christ. I am not dogmatic about the disciplines, but I do try to incorporate them into my life rhythms.

I've found wisdom and safety where, otherwise, pride and failure lurked. Take, for example, silence. The world seems forever noisy. Is there any real place of silence in our culture? And yet, pursuing silence produces quality spiritual fruit—especially in an age where not only noise reigns, but noise about one's self prevails.

For a moment, reflect on the words of the Desert Father Nilus:

The arrows of the enemy cannot touch someone who loves quiet. But those who wander about among crowds will often be wounded by them.[1]

Observing silence in our lives isn't just about turning off the noise. It's about keeping out of the noise itself: gossip at work, the success train, the inner circle. Too often we pursue noise in our vain attempts to find success or acceptance or to further our careers. It's easy to justify stepping into the fray. We want to be up on what's current. We want to seek justice for someone who's gone astray in the faith. The list goes on.

But Christ came so that we would not need to pursue the vainglory of the world. In him we find a resting place away from the trappings of the crowd. What better place to be than in the quiet strength of Jesus. Remember, traps wound—and the noise of the crowd is a beast of a trap.

Today's Prayer

Lord Jesus, keep me from the noise of the crowd by giving me your quiet, your rest, your strength.

The Sound of Silence   DAY 2

But the Lord was not in the fire.

1 Kings 19:12

If you want to really hear God, if you want to really experience the fullness of his joy, you will need to take a different path from the one the world offers. Come with me to Mount Horeb, the mount of God, where we find the prophet Elijah hiding in a cave in fear for his life. God tells him to stand at the mouth of the cave, for he was about to pass by. It is at this point that we read a most beautiful and haunting passage:

> And [God] said, "Go out and stand on the mount before the Lord." And behold, the Lord passed by, and a great and strong wind tore the mountains and broke in pieces the rocks before the Lord, but the Lord was not in the wind. And after the wind an earthquake, but the Lord was not in the earthquake. And after the earthquake a fire, but the Lord was not in the fire. And after the fire the sound of a low whisper.
>
> 1 Kings 19:11–12

What we are seeing in this passage is called a theophany, a visible manifestation of God to a human being. In the ancient Near East, theophanies were connected to battle. It was believed that the warrior gods would use thunderbolts (lightning or fire), the storm wind, and the trembling earth to fight for their people, terrifying the enemy. Baal, in particular, is imagined as holding a handful of thunderbolts. So it was believed in that culture that the gods operated and communicated by way of instilling terror into their enemies with tempestuous natural elements.

Theologians suggest Yahweh is also viewed as a warrior god in that he fights for his people. But as always, Yahweh has his own way of communicating. Unlike the ancient Near East gods who never articulated a plan for their so-called cultural involvement, Yahweh operated with a grand plan.

But the point in our discussion is not what God's plan was per se. Rather, it is how Yahweh communicated his plan to his people. This brings us to the mouth of the cave where Elijah stood. He stood there because God told him that he was about to pass by, and he was going to reveal his plan to Elijah. This awesome passing of God gives us insight into how God talks to us, right here and now.

When God passes by Elijah, three elements precede his actual passing: the storm wind, an earthquake, and a fire. Sound familiar? These are the very elements through which the ancient Near East gods were supposed to speak. And God uses them, but he's not in any of it! Instead, a fourth element follows: "the sound of a low whisper." The ESV rendering here is strikingly close to the Hebrew meaning. This phrase is not describing the sound of God's voice, as if it were like a gentle whisper.

Elijah hears the sound of silence.

The prophet encounters God's plan and direction not from the bombastic language of the ancient Near East gods, the language of culture, but from silence, literally.

There are two applications we can take from Elijah's brief encounter.

First, God does not work in ways that make sense in our culture. In fact, they look—or in this case, sound—completely different from what culture offers. Second, in order to hear God's direction in our lives, we need to cultivate space so that we can linger in the silence of God. We may expect him to communicate his plan in our common cultural mode, but this is not reality.

Today's Prayer

Lord Jesus, silence is scarce in this day and age. So, help me not only to find it but to find your voice of direction within it.

Undisturbed   DAY 3

Today's Prayer

Lord Jesus, lead me to a place of undisturbed quietness where love is not deserted if it does not itself depart. Let

*me see how these things pass away to give place to others
and how the universe in this lower order is constituted
out of all its parts.*

*Fix my dwelling with you, Lord. Let me entrust to the
truth whatever has come to my soul from the truth. I will
lose nothing.*

*May my decayed parts receive a new flowering, and all
my sickness be healed. All that is ebbing away from me
will be given fresh form and renewed.*[2]

Where He Calls Us   DAY 4

Very early in the morning, while it was still dark, Jesus got up,
left the house and went off to a solitary place, where he prayed.

Mark 1:35 NIV

In the book of Mark we see Jesus himself, on multiple occasions (Mark 1:19–39; 3:7–12; 6:30–56), pursuing a quiet place
to pray. In chapter six we see Jesus experiencing a full day of
teaching, feeding the five thousand, and eventually walking on
water in the middle of the night. But wedged in between those
events, Mark records that "after he had taken leave of them [the
disciples], he went up on the mountain to pray" (6:46).

The ultimate prayer scene with Jesus is in the garden of Geth-
semane. Think about the circumstances. Jesus goes with his
closest friends to a quiet place in the middle of the night. Jesus
leaves his friends and goes farther into the garden to pray in the
quiet and the shadows. Once alone, he pours out his supplication to his Father. He asks not to have to die.

Before the biggest day of his life, where do we find Jesus? On
his knees, sweating blood in a quiet place, praying.

It's in the silence that Jesus seeks God's face.

It's in the silence that Jesus approaches the biggest event of his life.

It's in the silence that Jesus gathers strength for the cross.

This is the silence he calls us to. This is the silence after the stormwind and the earthquake and the fire—the language of the culture. This is the context by which God reveals his direction for our lives. This is the context we see Jesus cultivating throughout his ministry. And this is the context from which Jesus gathered strength to face the insurmountable.

Today's Prayer

Lord Jesus, I am listening . . . in the quiet.

Shed the Noise   DAY 5

> Jesus withdrew with his disciples to the lake, and a large crowd from Galilee followed.
>
> Mark 3:7 NIV

Our culture has a way of drawing us into its *modus operandi.* Almost without knowing it, we expect God to work the way culture works—fast and opulent and obvious. But if we carry this expectation, we show our hand and reveal our own shallow understanding of God and how he works and communicates. We get so entrenched in the cultural language and so dialed in to the speed and immediacy that our childlike faith disappears. Instead, we wield an adult religion that falls vacant on our hearts and has little impact on the lives around us.

What will it take to get to that place of silence where we can actually find direction from God? What will it take to shed the culture and begin a new way of living, one marked by silence, childlike, and new every morning?[3]

Jesus encourages me. He chose to withdraw from the crowds right in the zenith of his ministry. He did not push on; he retreated into the quiet. Today, let us withdraw from the noise, into the quiet, and find God.

Today's Prayer

Lord Jesus, I am shedding the noise of culture today so that I can hear your gentle whisper.

Light

The Color of Light

> For anything that becomes visible is light.
>
> Ephesians 5:14

I read once that light is the color of transparency. Aristotle wrote it, and he had a lot of time on his hands. The thought befuddles, but I see its truth.

Light is immediacy—everywhere, but traveling nowhere. I look through the glass pane in my kitchen and see the chestnut and maple. I see them because transparency lets me. The window is not transparent, only a clear thing—transparency is the effect.

Transparency holds light and allows it to be everywhere. The trees outside shine into my eyes; visible, through transparency. Light is the color of transparency.

I read once that God stands within himself, like when he came down to Sinai and passed by Moses. He was at once the enveloping cloud of fire and light and commotion, and he was also the angel passing by the cowering Moses.

Befuddling, yes. But is it so hard to comprehend? We walk in his great cloud of commotion—a resonating world, throbbing with his glory, and pieces of heaven lying all over the place. And yet he walks within this glory because he lives inside of his mini human temples: us.

Glory within glory.

Today's Prayer

Lord Jesus, you are beautiful, and the light of your presence astounds me and moves me to worship you, Light of the world.

Light That Teaches Truth   DAY 2

I will turn the darkness before them into light. . . .

Isaiah 42:16

I pray for transparency. Not the unmitigated kind that lacks shame and thought. Rather, the kind that illuminates holy truth—that speaks to me in the quiet corners and helps me to see. Because of God, I am visible to myself, and see. Augustine always referred to God as light. "I bring my heart to you, Light that teaches truth," he wrote.[1]

To find God is to finally see, even if our human glass dims the view.

We cannot escape his light. It is everywhere and immediate. We cannot close our eyes in hopes of obliterating the light, like the child who shuts tight her eyes and comments on the darkness, all the while standing in the brilliance of the sun.

When the scales lift from our eyes, we find new lenses through which to see—our imaginations baptized. We gasp at color quicker. We tear at innocence longer. We *see.*

Today's Prayer

Lord Jesus, you are beautiful, and the light of your presence astounds me and moves me.

Celestial Contrast and Range   DAY 3

Today's Prayer

Lord Jesus, how I pray for sensation. Not the lusty, dim kind, but the fiery, consuming kind that reveals you to me—the light sparkling in the visible others walking around me. Aliens? No, they're just mini temples who wake again and again wanting to sense you so they can know you.

I thought I knew you until I stepped out and under the canopy of celestial contrast and range and beheld myself beneath the gulf, my form fixed and flailing in the doubt of my proportion and change. But then I spied the fixed radiance of your dot-beginning—more perfect than the circle, unique and true, the whole of your infinity and shape.

"Hosanna!" I yelled. "How I need saving. How I need help. How we all of us need you." And you gushed on me the immediacy of your brilliance. You ravished me in angelic fire and I cried because my bones no longer ached, my soul was no longer dry.

"Live!" you yelled back. "Revive, and be revived!" you bellowed.

Exact Radiance DAY 4

This is the message we have heard from him and declare to you:
God is light; in him there is no darkness at all.

1 John 1:5 NIV

If we say we have fellowship with him while we walk in dark-ness, we lie and do not practice the truth.

But if we walk in the light, as he is in the light, we have fellow-ship with one another, and the blood of Jesus his Son cleanses us from all sin. He is the radiance of the glory of God and the exact imprint of his nature, and he upholds the universe by the word of his power.[2]

What kind of God do we follow? He is light, and his lumi-nosity extends into the far reaches of the universe. He dispels darkness, dark forces, dark me, and dark you.

He is light in that to follow him is not to follow light, as if we were running in the shadows chasing light. Rather, it is to walk in the light itself—unable to notice the shadows for the brilliance.

Today's Prayer

Lord Jesus, I stand in awe of your magnificence. Your light eliminates darkness and heals my own darkness.

Post Script DAY 5

He makes his angels winds, and his ministers a flame of fire.

Hebrews 1:7

Who are you, God, that you command the winds and make them your legion armies like the angels surrounding your throne? Can you hear me, then, when I am muttering angry profanities in the morning over my cup of coffee, thinking no one can hear, and that no one cares? Is that you moving through the willow branches, playing with my daughters, making them laugh with their bellies?

Who are you, God, that you spark and crack into the night sky? You, drawing up into the cold oak boughs, listening to me strum the guitar and sing silly songs to the girls. Is that you splitting the winter sky with fire of dawn? Are you looking down upon me while I walk out into the gray air, now orange, now red, now day, and into your light?

If the winds can be your angels and if the fiery flames can be your ministers, then what can we be? Can we be your son, your daughter, your treasure—a jewel in your crown?

Who are you, God? Our flaming wind, our holy treasure, our sparking tree top and dancing branch.

Today's Prayer

Lord Jesus, there are days when I feel like even you don't care about me. Forgive me, but this is my honest heart. Draw me close to you today, precious Lord!

Trust

When I Can't Trust

Trust in the Lord with all your heart, and do not lean on your
own understanding.

Proverbs 3:5

The last ten days got me, like when a fighter receives an
uppercut in a fight. Within a seven-day span, the central
air-conditioner gave up the ghost and my laptop died. I had to
replace both. You can imagine the stress and expense. When the
air-conditioner failed, my family, including our new three-week-
old baby girl, was displaced. For two days we did whatever we
could to stay cool in the Atlanta heat.

Then I spent almost three days without a computer while the
Apple store completed a data transfer from the old machine to
the new one.

"This wasn't the best time for this to happen, God. In case
you didn't notice, things are tight right now: We've added a
third girl to the fold, and I have major deadlines."

79

This is my reality. Each aspect of my life—work, family, spiritual—affected in a very real and major way. But so what? How do my problems compare to yours? Does God even care? Why should I stress or sulk or throw oranges at God?

Doubt can emerge in the slightest crack of life. When the air-conditioner dies, your faith immediately receives a wake-up call: "Were we relying on our own intelligence and know-how to keep our house cool? If so, we're going to learn in the next couple of days how our faith should really be calibrated."

Well, the air-conditioner was fixed and my computer problems were solved rather easily, though it took some time. But where has my faith gone? Have I formed my life around the things I can control, leaving God on the margin, waiting for something to go wrong? Or will I surrender to him the things I think I control—like my money and my work and my family—and truly live like he's got me and everything about me in the palm of his hand?

Today's Prayer

Lord Jesus, why does it take uncontrollable events in life for me to realize I need you daily? Forgive me for trusting in my own ability to provide and fix. If I am following you truly, my responses to life's small calamities should look vastly different.

State of Love and Trust   DAY 2

> For I know the plans I have for you, declares the Lord, plans for welfare and not for evil, to give you a future and a hope.
>
> Jeremiah 29:11

I've been practicing the old hymn "I Surrender All" on my guitar lately. My heart trembles at the thought of leading that song in church. Will it be a true expression of how I feel? Can I surrender all, when life makes it so hard to trust?

"I will ever love and trust him," reads one line in the first verse. So much of life revolves around trust. To trust God I must shelve my penchant to take over and go it alone. To trust is to surrender our will, replacing it with the *belief* that the One who holds our trust is worthy of the task.

Today's Prayer

Lord Jesus, you are my strength and my shield. In you my heart trusts, and I am helped; my heart exults, and I give thanks to you.[1]

Altogether Trustworthy   DAY 3

Today's Prayer

Lord Jesus, you are altogether beautiful and trustworthy. You never fail. The prophets praised your faithfulness time and time again, even in the face of famine and death. Stretch out my trust like theirs, O Lord. Help me see your all-encompassing provision even when the bills and obligations stare me down. Help me to remember the profoundness of your faithfulness. Hem me in with all that you are, my Provider. I trust you.

Cutting Your Own Path   DAY 4

Behold, all you who kindle a fire, who equip yourselves with burning torches! Walk by the light of your fire, and by the torches that you have kindled! This you have from my hand: you shall lie down in torment.

Isaiah 50:11

I bumped around the corners of the kitchen, wheeling my bike through the back door and onto the deck. With my peanut butter and honey sandwich, my mini Moleskine, and my riding gloves, I set out on my "rise" ride.

I arrived at the trailhead just before dawn. The woods, empty. Normally I'd ride in the quiet of the morning. But all week I had been listening to *The Pilgrim's Regress* by C. S. Lewis. I continued listening to the audio book. After I plugged in my headphones, I tore off into the trees.

John, the main character in Lewis's allegory, is on a journey. He hopes to find an island far to the west—the source for his longing. But the journey winds its way through allegorical valleys and side trails and rough roads and cities—all representing varying philosophical influences of the times.

I descended Hare Trail with a "Woohoo!" When I started climbing again, after the creek crossing, my mind wandered.

Like John, all of us journey onward. I suppose for most of us, we too seek the shining island of heaven—experiencing it now already a bit, perhaps, and still not yet. And like John, we each must confront the Spirit of the Age. We must contemplate Wisdom and make decisions: *Which path will lead me to the island?*

But I wonder how many of us create our own pathways and try to bushwhack our way through this life? In our jobs, do we seek to leverage our way to the top? Beat the system by manipulating it for our own success?

Today's Prayer

Lord Jesus, I confess I have not been honest. I have found success, yes, but only by creating my own pathway. Forgive me for not trusting in the pathway you have laid out before me.

Flying Squirrel   DAY 5

You keep him in perfect peace whose mind is stayed on you, because he trusts in you. Trust in the Lord forever, for the Lord God is an everlasting rock.

Isaiah 26:3–4

In C. S. Lewis's *The Pilgrim's Regress*, John's problem was that he was unconvinced in his own mind. His journey was a path to belief. But as brothers and sisters in Christ, belief is behind us, really, and always before us. Our actions, the paths we take, the ones we create, stretch out ever before us.

There, biking in the woods, I flew down Flying Squirrel and looped back to White Tail Loop. I crossed the big stream and stood by the waterfall for a few moments.

"I *Am* the Way." The verse jumps out at me often. Yes, Christ is the way to salvation, to the island, but what does that imply regarding my business ethics? My family ethics? My political ethics?

As I loaded my bike on my Subaru, my thoughts fluttered to prayer. . . .

Today's Prayer

Lord Jesus, help me on the trail. Strengthen me over the logs and obstacles and through the rivers and all the hard junk. Keep me on your path, and forgive my bushwhacking ways. Onward!

The Long Pause

The Long Pause" is here to remind you to take a break from the normal routine and reflect, not only on this longer piece, but also on your own life rhythms. What needs to change? What needs to stop? What do you need more of? Use this long form piece, along with the reflection questions, as something to contemplate throughout the week.

I Want to Be Human

C. S. Lewis uses the phrase "the taste for the other" in his book *The Pilgrim's Regress* (the book I was reading earlier this week). John, the story's protagonist, possesses this *taste*. You and I possess it as well. It is the possessing of this "taste" for God, the God who is the "other," the God who is beyond all we can conceive or explain, that makes us human.

When we lose that taste, however, we cease to be human—our humanity dissipates into shadows. It is possible to exist in this world, to breathe, to eat and to work, and not be human. It isn't that we transmogrify into beasts with four legs, but that we become beasts within our souls.

J. R. R. Tolkien's character Gollum used to be a hobbit. But Gollum's taste for the ring of power turned him into a creature of shadow, bent low on his own lust. He ceases to possess the "taste." When, through the course of the story, he begins to help Frodo, he realizes that he himself—the Gollum—can thirst for something "other." He finds joy in serving Frodo, and only hate when he focuses on his lust—the ring, his precious. In the films, we see him turn ever so slightly more human when he serves.

This "taste" draws us out of ourselves. It's what makes fellowship with the divine possible. And all of us desire this, this fellowship with the divine. This taste is a self-giving love—it is what Gollum experienced even through his bent self. He found that he could give love.

Indeed, it is the nature of the universe, this self-giving love. It is the way of things: A seed falls from the tree, goes into the dark earth, and experiences a kind of death, only to surface as a shoot springing toward the sun.

A person who does not live from the viewpoint of the Christian story remains human only insofar as they allow the "taste for the other" to direct their charity. We see beautiful humans all over this earth—expressing self-giving love, reaching to satisfy that taste, yet not knowing the source of their hunger pain.

In C. S. Lewis's *The Great Divorce*, most of the people invited from hell into heaven rejected the invitation because they had things to do, or they were a big deal down in hell, or they didn't have time for the relationship offered to them. Again, Lewis's motif of death and taste reveals itself in that when we finally accept eternity into our lives, we must give of ourselves, releasing so much of the unhumanness that blackens our existence.

It would seem our humanity, though clothed in sophistication and the appearance of good, bends into shadow smiling and singing the praises of self—leveraging the good only to provide for personal lust.

Lewis suggests that Christians, however, journey as pilgrims. The taste draws them out of their selves and into others; it is the impetus for their relationship with God. Christians journey through pain and beauty in order to learn and understand self-giving. Their sojourn culminates with complete understanding, but not in this life. And so the tension of life, of pain and joy, of love and suffering, intermingle and frustrate.

"In love," writes Lewis, "we escape from our self into one another. In the moral sphere every act of justice or charity involves putting ourselves in the other person's place and thus transcending our own competitive particularity. . . . The primary impulse of each is to maintain and aggrandize himself. The secondary impulse is to go out of the self, to correct its provincialism and heal its loneliness. In love, in virtue, in the pursuit of knowledge, and in the reception of the arts, we are doing this."[1]

There is a living that is not unlike dying; the more often we die, the more human we become. For none of us is yet fully human. We sojourn to find that place where we can fill ourselves, to satisfy the desires we fail to satisfy. Jesus beckons you and me to come taste and see. And we turn toward the mirror of success, the mirror of power, the mirror of self.

I think, at times, we fear what Christ will do to us if we drink from his well of life, and so we drift off into the dark woods of self-fulfillment and look for our own water source.

We must never lose our taste for the *other*. We must never lose our thirst for God.

Reflection

1. Is it possible to do good in this world, all the while losing our humanness? Can you give an example? What is it that creeps in upon us that douses our desire for the other?
2. Life can sometimes numb, with its rhythms becoming mundane and droning. What can you do in these coming

months to combat the drone of sameness, the drone that drains your desire for the other?

3. Take some time and discuss your spiritual "state of drone" with a close friend. Really evaluate if you have let your good deeds go unchecked. Is there a spiritual affection pulling you onward in your journey to do good things?

4. Do you think it is satisfactory to help someone in a social justice context without giving them the truth of the gospel through your actual words?

Application

1. Take some real time this week to evaluate. Do you journal? Use your blog or your Moleskine or Composition notebook, or whatever is your tool of choice, and do the work of writing down your personal evaluations.

2. Find a friend or family member, a person you trust, and set up a time to discuss your evaluations. I love doing this with my wife. I also have a couple of friends I do this regularly with. More than likely your friend or loved one would love to chat about your personal evaluations, and it will no doubt inspire him or her to consider doing the same.

3. As you take time to "Pause" this week, find your favorite passage or chapter in the psalms, and dive into it each day. Find a centering point with your favorite encouraging psalm. Read some articles or commentaries about the chapter. Pull your pastor aside to ask some questions about it.

4. Finally, I encourage you to start prayer walking. I do this almost daily, and I must confess, I'd be lost without these times of pause and prayer. It doesn't have to be long, just a mile or two. Do it in your neighborhood, or drive to a trail. The point of the prayer walk is to unload. Give your anxiety to Christ. Begin your prayer with confession of your stress, your lingering sin, your failures. Then move on

from them—they're gone! Now, ask the Lord for strength and guidance and the patience to discover both. End your time with praise and thanksgiving. The walk doesn't have to be long, just enough to get away from your routine and find yourself in God's arms.

Intimacy

The Way Everlasting   DAY 1

> Those who obey God's commandments remain in fellowship
> with him, and he with them. And we know he lives in us because
> the Spirit he gave us lives in us.
>
> 1 John 3:24 NLT

A Pin Oak stands in my front yard, another in the back. They rise over the roof of my two-story house; their branches willow down in tangled rigidity.

In the spring the oaks receive their leaves last; in the fall they golden, but well after the other trees have lost their plumage. The brittle-browns fall throughout winter; a leafy remnant whips on when the spring push begins.

By mid-April the brittle-browns disappear, giving way to tiny glories. I watch the buds frost the mammoth skeletons, dressing them in God's finest.

In the summer the oaks blanket the ground with shade. When I prune them I always hold a couple of branches—their slender bones, dense and heavy.

How like the Pin Oak am I? Clinging to the old season until shaken by the Wind of God, thrashing me toward his glory.

We must, through life, embrace the storm of Christ. All of us live forever in a state of release and reaching—shedding the brittle-brown within us, clothing our dry bones in God's finest: *the way everlasting.*

This inner renewal looks like daily spring. When we gather as the family of God, we flutter and bounce, all glory given to Christ and his supremacy. When we in our homes love one another and entertain, we flutter and bounce, our hospitality and possessions reflecting the principles of release and reaching. We give without condition; we serve until we die.

How the Pin Oak catches the wind, first in its bare limbs, then in the applause of its plumage.

Today's Prayer

Lord Jesus, teach us to release and reach, that your *glory and* your *supremacy may blow through us into your world. All praise and glory to God. Amen.*

My Yawp Faith   DAY 2

Therefore I tell you, whatever you ask in prayer, believe that you have received it, and it will be yours.

Mark 11:24

I played in your land, O Lord, scoring the trail with my aggressive tread and steel steed. My bike lunged, wheelied, and billy-goated up and up. I pushed through switchbacks, laughing for the sheer dominance of man over earth. I laughed for the sheer joy of man communing with earth.

I jeep-rolled through the swollen creek, muddy with summer rain, and fell into the water atop river rocks and salamanders— and I hollered and spoke out damnation on the trail. I hollered and spoke out blessing on the trail. I climbed Heart-Attack Hill, praying out loud while the spike deer running next to me taunted me with graceful leaps.

And the prayer lifted, coming regular off my lips like friendship conversation, pub-like and frolicking, loving just the moment of sharing and the moments of laughing. I called out to you, "Change this reality. And, Lord, you can do *this*." I wasn't struck down for blasphemy. Instead, joy sprung from my brazen yet thankful words.

I was not silent in my prayer. In the open my words fell. The laurel heard me and rustled. The spike deer bounded back into the trees to tell his brethren. All of us raised our spirits. Oh, the wonder of hearing words spoken to God. Whitman's sheer "yawp" of our faith, of my faith.[1]

Am I barbaric, in the woods yelling out strange requests to God? Do I revel in something profane when I splash around in the mud and sing praise at the same time?

What is your quiet time like? I often pray on my bike. You may do it in the kitchen, whipping up the scrumptious fiddles for your lovies. Or maybe you whistle prayers on quiet walks down the lane, in the snow, in the spring, in the summer, in the leaves. I love to pray in the moments when I feel most alive. For me, my prayers quicken my spirit and I find boldness.

I am convinced that we pray not to change ourselves, but to change reality. We cannot bend God to us, yet he listens to our prayers. And he moves in our reality. He bends things to his righteous ones.

Today's Prayer

Lord Jesus, hear my prayers and move in my reality.

Fold It Back   DAY 3

Today's Prayer

Lord Jesus, can I be righteous for one day? Can you hear my prayer? It rises on thanksgiving and glows into the heavens with petition. I need you to stop the rain of pain and confusion today. And yet I need you to bring the deluge of you. I need you, I need you.

In my prayers I find delight. I fold it back and find you—the joy of my salvation. I am carving up this trail of life with my big wheels of hope and faith. You will bend for me and all I can do is sing.

Intimacy Through Prayer   DAY 4

Draw near to God, and he will draw near to you.

James 4:8

We do not seek intimacy for the sake of intimacy alone. Who sets out with intimacy as the goal of any relationship? It may be an unsaid goal, but we do not wake in the morning and say, "I can't wait to become more intimate with God today." Indeed, intimacy is not a destination at all. It is a journey.

We know when we are not intimate with God because we feel or sense the lack in our lives. On the other hand, we realize that when we live close to God's heart, something explodes daily in our heart—our desire is to know. Just like we want to know and be known by our friends and families, we desire to know and be known—maybe "feel known" is more accurate—by God.

Pain can drive us from intimacy. In such cases prayer is essential. We must not bottle ourselves up in our hurt and pain. No! We must pray. We must talk to a friend. We must pray.

Are you hurting? Pray. Do you feel great? Sing. Are you sick? Call the church leaders together to pray and anoint you with oil in the name of the Master. Believing-prayer will heal you, and Jesus will put you on your feet. And if you've sinned, you'll be forgiven—healed inside and out.

Make this your common practice: Confess your sins to each other and pray for each other so that you can live together whole and healed. The prayer of a person living right with God is something powerful to be reckoned with. Elijah, for instance, human just like us, prayed hard that it wouldn't rain, and it didn't—not a drop for three and a half years. Then he prayed that it would rain, and it did. The showers came and everything started growing again.

James 5:13–18 THE MESSAGE

Today's Prayer

Lord Jesus, I want to know you. And I want to feel like you know me.

Heaven and Earth   DAY 5

But seek first the kingdom of God and his righteousness, and all these things will be added to you.

Matthew 6:33

The hosanna chorus rings out and my praise stretches to meet it. In heaven the cherubim serve the throne room of God, protecting with fire. But why does God need protection? It is a mystery, as mysterious as the winged creatures themselves—angelic, human, animal. The composite and holy beings guard with swords ablaze. They are the keepers of the Tree of Life and the God of life. The mystery of heaven and the God who inhabits constantly unfolds.

Is this the kingdom I am to seek? Is it this holy kingdom of gryphons and swords, magic trees and throne rooms?

It is, in fact, this magic, this fire. For the kingdom on earth exists and spreads through the bloody ethic of Christ and his cross and his sin-destroying death. What else but magic can account for a life lived prostrate, dying to others, dying to self? It is as odd as the beast-angel-cherubim with its flaming sword hovering around the presence of God as they are dazzled into ephemeral wonder by the song of light, which is the very kingdom of God.

And Christ represents this kingdom on earth—a wholly different kind of kingdom, just like the different and eccentric cherubim, a wholly new and thriving kingdom, just like the incandescent sword-guard-cherubim protecting a tree that can give eternal life.

Yes, truly we live in a magic kingdom. Not a novel kind of magic, but a heavenly kind—a mythical kind that only translates into an earthly life that looks like it belongs on this planet yet acts as though it belongs in a world where fiery-sword-wielding gryphons protect a God who needs no protecting and a tree no one can access this side of eternity.

Today's Prayer

Lord Jesus, I am seeking your kingdom because I know that you will not let me down. You will illuminate this world with your light shining right through me.

Anxiety

Wildflowers and Wormwood   DAY 1

> Do not be anxious about anything.
> Philippians 4:6

C. S. Lewis wrote an odd little book called *The Screwtape Letters*.[1] It is a collection of correspondences between an elder demon named Screwtape and his apprentice (and nephew), Wormwood. Uncle Screwtape encourages his nephew to use subtle devices as he torments his subject.

Sometimes Wormwood crawls into my brain and begins to whisper obscenities and lies. "Do more," he says. "It's not enough and you'll probably fail. You need more money. You need more accomplishments. You need . . . you must . . . go and get."

How do I respond? In my weakness, I fuss and worry.

I like to think of myself as not much of a fusser. Truth is, in the quiet my heart beats fast and I lie awake. *Do you really have me, Lord?*

Then Paul sneaks up beside me and says:

95

Don't fret or worry. Instead of worrying, pray. Let petitions and praises shape your worries into prayers, letting God know your concerns. Before you know it, a sense of God's wholeness, everything coming together for good, will come and settle you down. It's wonderful what happens when Christ displaces worry at the center of your life.

Philippians 4:6–7 The Message

Today's Prayer

Lord Jesus, why do I fret? Today I give it all to you. No fretting.

Thanksgiving   DAY 2

But in everything by prayer and supplication with thanksgiving let your requests be made known to God.

Philippians 4:6

Jesus climbs next to me and agrees with Paul's words above. "Well said, Paul," he says. "Tim, don't fuss about what's on the table at mealtimes or if the clothes in your closet are in fashion. There is far more to your inner life than the food you put in your stomach, more to your outer appearance than the clothes you hang on your body.

"Look at the ravens, free and unfettered, not tied down to a job description, carefree in the care of God. And you count far more.

"Has anyone by fussing before the mirror ever gotten taller by so much as an inch? If fussing can't even do that, why fuss at all?

"Walk into the fields and look at the wildflowers. They don't fuss with their appearance—but have you ever seen color and design quite like it? The ten best-dressed men and women in the country look shabby alongside them.

"If God, my Father, gives such attention to the wildflowers, most of them never even seen, don't you think he'll attend to you, take pride in you, do his best for you?

"What I'm trying to do here is get you to relax, not be so preoccupied with getting so you can respond to God's giving. People who don't know God and the way he works fuss over these things, but you know both God and how he works. Steep yourself in God-reality, God-initiative, God-provisions. You'll find all your everyday human concerns will be met."[2]

Today's Prayer
Lord Jesus, show me your reality. I want to love and be concerned about the things that matter most to you.

Simple   DAY 3

Today's Prayer
Lord Jesus, I want to simplify. It seems in order to do so is to bypass the anxious thoughts and notions clouding my mind and disrupting my heart. I cannot pray like I should. I struggle to find quiet. Today, give me the victory of your glory. You shine through my quivering thoughts—shine today, for me, again.

Look Up   DAY 4

And the peace of God, which surpasses all understanding, will guard your hearts and your minds in Christ Jesus.

Philippians 4:7

In my previous conversation with Jesus and Paul, Jesus compelled me (and all of us) to relax. Paul then added some concluding remarks:

"Tim," he reminded me, "this is how we should live if we follow Jesus. So, if you're serious about living this new resurrection life with Christ, act like it. Pursue the things over which Christ presides.

"Don't shuffle along, eyes to the ground, absorbed with the things right in front of you. Look up, and be alert to what is going on around Christ—that's where the action is. See things from his perspective."[3]

Today's Prayer

Lord Jesus, my God, I need these words. I need to settle down. I need to relax in the peace of Christ.

No More   DAY 5

> I can do all things through him who strengthens me.
>
> Philippians 4:13

Do not lose heart, brothers and sisters. Though anxiety can overwhelm, God's love lofts greater and higher—up into the sky, more immense and with a glory that smashes the world's anxiety. This is not some battle we should worry about. What does worry get us, anyway? A headache? Some heartache?

Today is a day of courage, my friends. I am not overstating. For it will take constant courage to concentrate on the Holy One and what he's doing. He wants our hearts, and when he gets them, he is faithful and just, and will make our hearts soar. So take comfort on this final day of the workweek. He is greater. He can do it all. And he is the One from whom we find our own strength.

Today's Prayer

Lord Jesus, I am not worrying about "this" anymore. Your strength is sufficient.

Surrender

No More Rebellion

> For the wages of sin is death, but the free gift of God is eternal life in Christ Jesus our Lord.
>
> Romans 6:23

The human condition stems from rebellion. In Eden, rebellion broke perfection and shattered the world. We inherited the rebellion. Humankind lives now as hardened rebels, crashing into one another on planet earth. The pieces from our collisions stab and hurt us.

As rebels, our sentence is guilty, death (Romans 6:23). We wince at this truth. Some even speak of our condition as brokenness—and we are broken, true indeed. Brokenness, however, stands as a result of rebellion. Yes, you and I are broken, but we are sinners, rebels, first. We should take care not to remove culpability (responsibility for a wrong) from sin, lest the point of salvation moves from being about Christ to being about our own desire for wholeness.

"Our motive for surrender should not be for any personal gain at all," writes Oswald Chambers. "We have become so self-centered that we go to God only for something from him, and not for God himself."[1]

Salvation is not about us and not about our desire to be whole. It is about Christ himself. Christ is the Way, and that *Way* led an uprising in Jerusalem. Nationals desired a ruling messiah. But they received the Messiah—Immanuel. God walked among us and offered a way out of rebellion.

Perhaps the unsaved person attending on Sunday desires another way. The brokenness and confusion and ultimate letdown of a world gone to hell overwhelms her heart. What would she want—need to hear and see from us, the family of God?

Imagine Jesus taking the stage on Sunday, addressing us all—rebel-saints.

"You, my son, my daughter, you wandered in here confused. You're looking for something else, something *other* than what the world offers.

"But you can't get past the brokenness, the disappointment, the pain. I want to tell you something. I fed the five thousand to show you how I alone can provide for all your needs. I walked on water to show you what it takes to follow me—you must step out of your boat and walk in the way most unknown.

"I healed the blind so you could see me. I held off the stone-throwers so you could turn from the way of pain and follow me.

"This morning you look for a way. I am the Way. In this Way you'll find righteousness, 'a righteousness from God that comes through faith in me to all who believe.'

"Believe in me today. Do a one-eighty on the path you're on and yoke up with me—it's easy, the burden is light. It's light because I carry it for you."

We fall into wholeness on the other side of the cross, the empty tomb. We step into wholeness by way of belief, and that step is the most dangerous. And it is also the most glorious.

"Genuine total surrender is a personal sovereign preference for Jesus Christ himself," says Chambers.[2]

Today's Prayer

Lord Jesus, I am rebel, but you have turned me into saint. Thank you for your grace and kindness.

Our Response to Wholeness   DAY 2

Let us draw near with a true heart in full assurance of faith, with our hearts sprinkled clean from an evil conscience and our bodies washed with pure water. Let us hold fast the confession of our hope without wavering, for he who promised is faithful. And let us consider how to stir up one another to love and good works, not neglecting to meet together, as is the habit of some, but encouraging one another, and all the more as you see the Day drawing near.

Hebrews 10:22–25

Today, dear reader, pray through the following reflection. Make it personal to you.

O sweet Lord, who is like you? You are the exact radiance of God's glory. You are mindful of me—and how easily I forget this fact! Your heavenly Father perfected you through suffering so that by grace you might taste death for me. And yet you are not ashamed of me, Lord. You even call me brother (sister)!

And what a beautiful family, indeed! You shared in my humanity, so you know what this flesh feels like—suffocating and feeble. I hear your voice, Lord, and I run to you. Keep me from further rebellion. I want to enter into your place of rest. I want to taste and see your glory here in the present life and in the life to come.

Lord, you are my High Priest. You make intercession for me. Your blood not only gives me salvation, it gives me confidence to live right now as your co-heir, bringing your brilliance into all my endeavors.

It is because of this confidence that the writer of Hebrews beckons me and all my Christian brothers and sisters to draw near to you, to grip hope with iron firsts, never to let go, to encourage the family of God toward love and good deeds, and to keep meeting together for worship and fellowship. For you are coming soon!

Today's Prayer

Lord Jesus, I look forward to the wholeness you bring, and I live toward that wholeness today as I encourage others, hope for glory, live brilliantly, and meet with your Family.

The Skull   DAY 3

Today's Prayer

Lord Jesus, today I remember Golgotha. The day you took all the sin of the world upon yourself; the day you became sin—you became a whore, a murderer, a thief, a liar, a swindler, an adulterer . . . and the Father turned from you. Darkness covered the earth. The temple veil ripped. The dead woke and proclaimed you as the Son of God.

On this day, Lord, you ended the rebellion and paved the way back to glory through the crimson wood and dirt on the Place of a Skull. Salvation draws us to you. It changed the world. For you yourself are our salvation—our way into light.

Relationship Desolation   DAY 4

Submit yourselves therefore to God. Resist the devil, and he
will flee from you.

James 4:7

As we reflected earlier this week, our brokenness is a by-product of sin. Hurt and pain (brokenness), however, come from human rebellion, against one another and against God. We live as hardened rebels crashing into one another. The pieces from our collisions stab and hurt us, as well as those we love. Our hurt and brokenness can hurt others when we live from that hurt. Guilt, accumulated from our life pain, ruins most of us.

Guilt is also the position we take before God because of sin. As guilty rebels before God, our wage is death. But Christ's once-and-for-all sacrifice atones for our sin, past and present. It allows us to live, not in guilt, which causes us to hurt others and ourselves, but to live in the freedom of willful obedience to God.

In my guilt I lash out. When I feel "found out" by God, I tend to treat others harshly. The rebel in me rears his head and wants to destroy. When I was a boy, destroying meant something physical. Now, as a man, destroying manifests itself in the desolation of relationships.

How does guilt affect your behavior?

Today's Prayer

Lord Jesus, how can I, when I am so far into the desolation, submit? I want to learn to surrender before I fall into desolation, because today this black pit seems inescapable. Hear me, Lord.

Brazen Fist   DAY 5

And going a little farther, he fell on the ground and prayed that,
if it were possible, the hour might pass from him. And he said,
"Abba, Father, all things are possible for you. Remove this cup
from me. Yet not what I will, but what you will."

Mark 14:35–36

Y ou and I stand accused, responsible for our sin for which
Jesus calls us to repent. When we fully turn from sin, we
move away from a guilty life to one of grace, forgiveness, and
unmitigated love.

In truth, our human status before God is one of guilt. We do
not exist as crumbled men and women from birth. We stand
like a brazen fist, taut and wrangled and clinched against one
another and against God. We break one another, crashing into
the lives of others and destroying hearts. We can destroy with
ease because both objects are hard yet fragile, easily broken like
glass panes. Sin hardens us; *we* break us.

But—what a blessed conjunction! Yes, we stand accused but
not condemned! We wake in death but are raised each morning
into life—his life, the life of Christ Jesus. He took the guilt and
sent it into desolation. He took our brazen fists and relaxed
them, healed them, held them. His willingness to submit to
God the Father's will established a true and beautiful route to
glory: his own pure death.

Christ submitted and surrendered so that we could as well.
He took the guilt so that we could stand free, ready to fly.

Today's Prayer

Lord Jesus, thank you for your willingness to surrender.
You are my model, my encouragement, my King!

Humility

Only the Lowly

> I tell you the truth, whoever does not receive the kingdom of God like a child will never enter it.
>
> Luke 18:17 NET

What does it mean to have childlike faith?

When I read verses in the New Testament where Jesus says that I must become "like a child" or that if I don't "receive the kingdom of God like a child" then I can't enter it, my mind immediately thinks that I must become innocent like a child.

Though we can learn much from the innocence of children, Jesus is not referring to that characteristic here.

The greatest in the kingdom is the person who assumes the lowliest position within a culture. It's easy for us to ascribe characteristics of secular greatness to spiritual greatness, because greatness in our society is quantifiable. In the Greco-Roman culture, a child was at the bottom of the pecking order. What are we to assume then? What is our prayer?

Today's Prayer

Lord Jesus, I want to become lowly as a child so that my faith will shine like the sun—so that I will receive your kingdom.

Depend on Me   DAY 2

Blessed is the man who makes the Lord his trust, who does not turn to the proud, to those who go astray after a lie!

Psalm 40:4

In yesterday's reading, we were reminded of the idea Christ constantly drove home: If you want to be great, you must be the least. These are hard words to live by in a culture where personal ambition and celebrity culture mix into a concoction of pride and envy.

Another aspect to consider, then, is dependence. Remember the people of Shinar. They looked at what they had built with their own hands. Their culture was great and beautiful, why did they need God? So they constructed a tower—the Tower of Babel. In the pride of their self-sufficiency they excluded God, so God confused and scattered them.

Think about how dependent a child is upon her parents. She cannot help but to trust. She cannot help but to wait for her sustenance. She trusts that she will be comforted and laid to rest in a safe shelter.

Today's Prayer

Lord Jesus, I know you hold me—you have me in the palms of your hands. I want to depend on you first, and not the works of my own hands.

Weave Into Me   DAY 3

Today's Prayer

Lord Jesus, weave into me. Leave your trace elements, like minerals feeding my soul. I ram and rake, pushing through the thistle-brush of the daily muck. Pride does not scribble. It writes through me, and on me, in the cuts of self-sufficiency.

Give me heavenly bread. I want to believe in the magic food of wilderness. For my flesh bleeds and my body aches—such is life lived unto the self.

I eat you, my bread and portion. You trace into me and weave guilt-erasing light. Now I can breathe. I can cling and sing to you. Amen.

Wilderness Bread   DAY 4

Truly, truly, I say to you, whoever believes has eternal life. I am the bread of life. Your fathers ate the manna in the wilderness, and they died. This is the bread that comes down from heaven, so that one may eat of it and not die.

John 6:47–50

Have you become self-sufficient? Have I? Have we done well for ourselves—have we created the perfect scenario for our careers to soar—and yet forgotten God? Could we actually be enjoying a success that God allowed but has not blessed?

I do not think Jesus was trying to be cute when he beckoned the children to his side. I think it was a vivid way to communicate a hard truth to his disciples: "Are you fully dependent upon me, so much so to trust me for your sustenance and your very life? Are you willing to become low so that I might lift you high?"

Today's Prayer

Lord Jesus, how do I answer these questions without condemning myself? I will sit in the silence of your presence and wait to be lifted high.

My Worldly-Entanglement-Shedding Faith DAY 5

Apart from me you can do nothing.

John 15:5

Turns out, a childlike faith is tough. It's a worldly-entanglement-shedding faith that reverses the cultural expectation of greatness. Today it is enough to meditate on the words of Jesus above.

True humility, according to Richard Foster, is understanding the truth about reality and acting accordingly. In the case of Christ, our reality is we are nothing without him. Only when we admit this will we find ourselves at the beginning point of the long and beautiful road of humility.

Today's Prayer

Lord Jesus, you are my everything.

Mystery

All Things Considered DAY 1

The secret things belong to the Lord our God.
Deuteronomy 29:29

If you have lost your sense of mystery, then do what you must to retrieve it. Mystery emerges in the most simple of places. Most often it manifests itself in reaction to the beauty and goodness encountered in our everyday life—through feelings of awe and wonder, events that elicit thanksgiving.

The late German theologian Hans Urs von Balthasar wrote:

All things can be considered in two ways: as fact and as mystery. Simple people, farmers for instance, can often integrate both ways in a lovely harmony. In children it would for the most part be easy to develop a sense of mystery; but teachers and parents can seldom generate enough humility to speak of it.[1]

Keeping and cultivating a sense of mystery protects against pride and keeps us as children before the Lord. As I think through how to keep mystery in my life, three pathways emerge.

Pace of Life. Evaluate your everyday—your context. Mystery reveals itself to the simple because their pace of life allows them to encounter more. The to and fro of busyness can too often blind us with a false sense of efficiency and success.

Slow down and see life. If you do, mystery will blindside you daily and in the most uncommon of ways.

Offering of Praise. Celebrate the simple things. Celebrate the beautiful things. "Sing joyfully to the Lord, you righteous; it is fitting for the upright to praise him" (Psalm 33:1 NIV).

As God's children it makes sense to celebrate him for all that he has done and will do. "Praise not merely expresses but completes the enjoyment," writes C. S. Lewis.[2]

A Thankful Heart. Thankfulness marks the contented heart. Not so the prideful heart. Pride desires more—and even more, it bears the insatiable mark of avarice. When we say thank-you to God, we live in the contentment of his grace-blessing.

Today's Prayer

Lord Jesus, forgive me for not offering more praise and thanksgiving, and help me to pace myself better. These three things I seek. I want to leave room for your mystery.

Delight   DAY 2

Send out your light and your truth; let them lead me; let them bring me to your holy hill and to your dwelling! Then I will go to the altar of God, to God my exceeding joy, and I will praise you with the lyre, O God, my God.

Psalm 43:3–4

Today I found several dahlia blossoms collected in the crook of one of our little sweetgum trees in the backyard. My girls leave little faerie offerings like that all over the landscape; I love finding these surprises while I'm pruning and weeding.

Their delight reminds me of the importance of spiritual mystery in my life. It slows me down so I can feel the cool spring air lingering on the late spring breeze. It reopens my eyes to behold his glory I so often miss because of a godless frantic pace.

And in that time of glory and easeful stride I am able to catch my breath and whisper, "Thank you, Jesus."

Today's Prayer

Lord Jesus, thank you for your unfathomable depth. I daily long to lose myself in your mystery.

Safe in the Unknown   DAY 3

Today's Prayer

Lord Jesus, having the glory of God—its radiance like a most rare jewel, like a jasper, clear as crystal[3]—is like having the sunlight given to me, something I cannot possess but that will always provide me warmth. I do not understand how it works or what sustains it, but I am content to bask in its rays. The sun envelops the day as you envelop me, and I am comforted and at peace with both.

Beauty Beckons Mystery DAY 4

Now to him who is able to strengthen you according to my gospel and the preaching of Jesus Christ, according to the revelation of the mystery that was kept secret for long ages.

Romans 16:25

What does beauty show us? To C. S. Lewis, beauty pointed to another place. "The books or the music in which we thought the beauty was located will betray us if we trust them," writes Lewis, "it was not in them, it only came through them, and what came through them was longing."

Our poetry and photographs, our music and films, stir us with a beauty we struggle to communicate—mystery. "They are not the thing itself," Lewis continues. "They are only the scent of a flower we have not found, the echo of a tune we have not heard, news from a country we have never yet visited."[4]

The apologetic of beauty seems abstract. Does the pointing finger of beauty finally rest on God himself? Can we really transpose the feelings we receive when we experience beauty into foundational beliefs—and belief in God, no less? I think these questions matter, but not for our reflection today.

By pursuing the beautiful in life, we invite mystery. God makes himself known in all creation, and yet the more time I spend planting flowers with my daughters, for example, the more I find his character revealed; not only in the visual beauty of the flowers themselves, but in how they bring me and the girls together and the life principles we learn from planting and growing. We discover the mystery of life and trace it to a God who cares enough about his children to reveal himself in the glory of pansies and black-eyed Susans.

Today's Prayer

Lord Jesus, I want to learn more about you. I am seeking the beauty around me to discover and unravel the mystery of you.

Made for Beauty, Made for Mystery   DAY 5

The glory that you have given me I have given to them.

John 17:22

We watch the sun set. It stirs a desire within us. We cannot quite describe the desire—we want some part of the experience. But what? C. S. Lewis says we don't want the sunset itself. Rather, we want to crawl inside of it and wash ourselves with whatever it is behind the sunset—an experience or interaction with its Creator.

Studies in science tell us our brains are hardwired for belief. God made us with the ability to desire that which cannot always be seen or fully known. "If I find in myself a desire which no experience in this world can satisfy," says Lewis in *Mere Christianity*, "the most probable explanation is that I was made for another world."[5]

In a BBC feature, Ben Quash, professor of Christianity and the Arts at King's College London, said beauty is known best when it is giving the sense of home and communion. We find echoes of Lewis here, for Lewis always seems to be reaching for home in his writings, while at the same time aiming us at the sunset—content to leave us in the arms of longing.

Do you feel the pull of another world? When you encounter the mysterious and the beautiful, do you also experience a peace in knowing that Jesus is showing himself to you? I feel at home in mystery, but it seems many Christians think mystery and the lack of answers uncomfortable. I think God gives us mystery so that we stay humble, so that we constantly thirst for him, so that we continually find delight.

Today's Prayer

Lord Jesus, I love how you unfold your truth in the mystery of your glory. Thank you for thinking of me enough to delight my senses with all you are.

Devotion

Expensive Love

Why wasn't this oil sold and the money given to the poor? It would have easily brought three hundred silver pieces.

John 12:4–6 THE MESSAGE

Christmas never ends, in my mind. I am always struck by its significance. Since the garden fallout, God has pursued his children. At Christmas we find him among us. Immanuel.

Jesus' birth marks the advent of a thirty-three-year period of God living among mankind—a staggering reality.

But Christmas does not represent the whole story, it only begins it. Indeed, we find the climax of this story in the Passion Week of Jesus and then punctuated by a horrific death scene at the hill of the skull. Christianity views this scene as the culmination of Jesus' work on earth, bringing salvation to mankind. The early church instituted a period of weeks leading up to the execution and resurrection of Jesus as Lent.

During Lent, many Christians evidence their devotion to Jesus by giving up something. I wonder how many of us, though, have given up our entire salary or have spent intimate time with Jesus—baring the deepest secrets of our souls to him.

John the Beloved shares a riveting scene in his gospel account. I'm sure you've heard it at least once a year. That might be a good thing. It might also cause you (as it does me) to pass over the passage's beauty and witness. Eugene Peterson paints the scene in *The Message* like this:

> Six days before Passover, Jesus entered Bethany where Lazarus, so recently raised from the dead, was living. Lazarus and his sisters invited Jesus to dinner at their home. Martha served. Lazarus was one of those sitting at the table with them. Mary came in with a jar of very expensive aromatic oils, anointed and massaged Jesus' feet, and then wiped them with her hair. The fragrance of the oils filled the house.
>
> John 12:1–3

Judas responds to Mary's seemingly frivolous act of waste with indignation, and feigns compassion for the poor to hide his own greed. Jesus rebukes him, "Let her alone. She's anticipating and honoring the day of my burial. You always have the poor with you. You don't always have me."

Jesus' comments do not direct us to treat the poor as secondary. Rather, he's emphasizing the gravity of Mary's action: an act of pure and unadulterated devotion.

Today's Prayer

Lord Jesus, have I become sedentary in my devotion for you? Do I care about the wrong things when I should be focusing real effort on knowing you more intimately and learning what it means to love you? Help me to learn from Judas, here. May I never feign spirituality in order to look good in the world's eyes.

Cultural Scandal   DAY 2

Then Mary took a twelve-ounce jar of expensive perfume made
from essence of nard, and she anointed Jesus' feet with it, wiping
his feet with her hair. The house was filled with the fragrance.

John 12:3 NLT

Mary dumped a year's wages' worth of perfume on Jesus.
Some scholars think she doused him from head to toe.
Then, in an act of cultural scandal, she let down "the tresses of
her hair" and wiped the perfume from his feet. Mary's gesture
carried an intimate and even sexual connotation within Jewish
culture (it was considered inappropriate for women to let their
hair down in front of men) and revealed her naked devotion to
her Savior.

Did Jesus stop her? No. He thought it good. He recognized
her devotion, and a couple of millennia later, so do we . . . Or
do we?

I cannot fully grasp Mary's act—the intimacy of it, the lavish expenditure of it. I think we discover spiritual benefits when
we observe Lent. But why do I participate, really? Why do you?
How devoted are we to Jesus the rest of the year? Maybe Advent
gives us an excuse to get our priorities straight, making up for
the months after Lent. And what of Jesus? Why does he allow
this woman to perform such an intimate act?

Today's Prayer

*Lord Jesus, how real is my devotion—how intimate, how
much does it cost me? Forgive me for caring too much
about what others might think if I give myself to you in
the way my heart truly desires.*

No More Cheap Christianity   DAY 3

Today's Prayer

Lord Jesus, have I cheapened what it means to follow you by devotion of nonchalance? How quick I am to forget the gift of life you gave to me on the cross. Forgive me for thinking too much of religious practices, and help me to show my devotion—not by how well I "perform" during Lent or Advent, but by the consistency of a life lived to the praise of your glorious grace.

Lead me into the path of naked devotion as I learn what it means to give my love in ways that actually cost me something. Enough of this cheap Christianity—I want you, all of you, every day. I love you, my Beloved, my Christ.

Unexpected Savior   DAY 4

Many in the crowd had seen Jesus call Lazarus from the tomb, raising him from the dead, and they were telling others about it. That was the reason so many went out to meet him—because they had heard about this miraculous sign.

John 12:17–18 NLT

It turns out Jesus is not whom the people expected. In the post-hoopla of Lazarus's resurrection, the people were frenzied, shouting old Hebrew praises and laying palm branches down in front of Jesus. They wanted a national ruler, a king. They wanted their oppression ended. They wanted. They wanted.

Jesus grabbed a young donkey, an act that spoke louder than words: "I'm not *that* guy. I'm something far greater."

Mary saw that "something," and her selfless act gives you and me a picture of deep devotion that "signifies the utmost in self-humbling devotion and love, regardless of the cost or of what others might think."[1] Maybe it's not what we give up during Lent, but *who* we give up for all time—namely, ourselves.

Do we value Jesus more than our work, more than our influence? Are we waiting at his feet, just *being*? Or are we too busy, off in a hurry? Do we cling to his Word regardless of what others say or think?

Today's Prayer

Lord Jesus, may we humbly adore you, our Savior and King, in the weeks leading to Easter, but may it extend into and throughout every fabric of our lives.

Naked Devotion   DAY 5

Listen carefully: Unless a grain of wheat is buried in the ground, dead to the world, it is never any more than a grain of wheat. But if it is buried, it sprouts and reproduces itself many times over. In the same way, anyone who holds on to life just as it is destroys that life. But if you let it go, reckless in your love, you'll have it forever, real and eternal.

John 12:24–25 THE MESSAGE

Is my grip on this world too tight, Lord? Have I missed the signs that tell me my love and devotion for you are fading?

I remember finding you when I was a boy and asking you into my heart. That little boy's prayer seems a lifetime away from me now. I wonder if at that point I took the seed of your love and hid it away—so thankful for eternal life that I neglected the eternal right here and now.

But then I remember times in my life when I sacrificed for a friend or answered the prodding of your Holy Spirit—how that love blossomed then and touched so many others. That is who I want to be: the devoted farmer of the spiritual and heavenly, allowing my love for you to grow in the cool soil, compelled to climb into the air by the warmth of your brilliance.

I want to be reckless in my love for you. I want to not care what the people in church think of me when I sing to you. I want to speak your truth unafraid in a world that longs for more—that longs for you.

Today's Prayer

Lord Jesus, the more I grow in faith and devotion I am able to see further into your grace. I am walking out on the waters of devotion. Keep me from drowning. Raise me up, Lord, as I proclaim your glory through my life, my love, my all.

Family

The Family Business

> So then you are no longer strangers and aliens, but you are fellow
> citizens with the saints and members of the household of God.
>
> Ephesians 2:19

Let us talk plainly. Our "family" experiences range somewhere between the Cleavers and the Simpsons. From pie-in-the-sky to serious dysfunction, the idea of family can mean many things to many people. I grew up a pastor's son, with four siblings. We played, we laughed, we fought, we hugged, and we played some more.

Though we experienced our fair share of drama, my family still clings to the tight bonds we formed as children—we are still close friends and love each other with a fierce kind of love. So when I write about family, I am, obviously, projecting a bit of my context on this.

How *should* a family function? I think you and I know in our hearts how a family ought to act, how a family ought to treat one another. Why else would we struggle with baggage left undone from our family relationships and wince from the hurts that come from familial injustice? Because we know it should not be like that—a family sticks together, a family helps one another, a family forgives. A family loves without condition, a family does not betray, a family seeks the good for all, a family cries together. We inherently know how a family *should* work, but we all have our varying stories of how what "should work" fails.

But what about our other family, dare I say our real family? You know the one, the family of God.

Today's Prayer

Lord Jesus, guide my heart and mind this week as I consider what it means to be part of the family of God.

Family of God   DAY 2

Beloved, let us love one another: for love is of God; and every one that loveth is born of God, and knoweth God.

1 John 4:7 KJV

I know we like to talk about the body of Christ as the controlling metaphor for the universal collection of the saints. But I prefer *family* as that metaphor. One of my professors in graduate school helped me realize that God, from creation forward, is building a family. He comes after us like a true father should—his children are lost, and he will find them—no matter the cost.

What if we did our utmost to apply the family metaphor to our Sunday worship gatherings, to our interactions with one another at church and in the community and in the public square, and to how we deal with confrontations with one another? Would we be so quick to skewer Christian leaders in the public square (i.e., blogs, news services) regardless of their perceived guilt? Or would we treat accountability as family business, private and loving, yet stern—using Matthew 18 as our guide on how to confront? Would we cheapen our Sunday gatherings with surface talk so we can exit as quickly as possible, or would we get right to it and talk honestly with one another—using our time to encourage one another by discussing how God is at work on our lives and what we are learning?

When I gather with my siblings, the love runs deep. We laugh and play, but we also discuss real issues, our hurts and victories, and our needs. What if I treated you like my sister when I saw you on Sunday? How many of us would leave church encouraged, feeling loved and cared for, supported and cheered on by our family?

Today's Prayer

Lord Jesus, I want so badly to be a sister/brother to those in my church. Bless our church family and help us love one another like you love us.

My Intimate Father   DAY 3

Today's Prayer

Lord Jesus, I love being part of your family. Show me how your family works. Teach me how your family loves. And even as I pray this, I can see your one-of-a-kind Son, Jesus. He showed me.

He lived with his disciples, was their friend, ate with them, prayed with them, cried with them, laughed with them—intimacy was his way, and it shall be mine as well.

John the Beloved reminds us, "You belong to God, my dear children" (1 John 4:4 NLT). How beautiful to think that by coming to Jesus I am coming home. What is more, I belong to him—I am his possession. How I long to see you, God, to see my Father. But when I love the family of God, I do see you, for no one can see you and live. And yet you tell us to love one another, and by so doing, we will see you, for you will dwell deeply within us and show us your most perfect way.

Our Epic   DAY 4

By yourself you're unprotected. With a friend you can face the worst. Can you round up a third? A three-stranded rope isn't easily snapped.

Ecclesiastes 4:12 THE MESSAGE

In a culture that prizes the individual, it is easy to forget that strength to make it through every day, every trial, every disappointment comes from others. King Solomon included this "saying" (today's verse) in his book of wisdom, but it was not original to him; it was a common axiom in the ancient Near East.

In the *Epic of Gilgamesh*, there is a scene where Gilgamesh and his friend Enkidu take fifty men and travel to the "the land of the living" (literally, a land of cedar trees) where Gilgamesh falls into troubled sleep. Worried for his friend, Enkidu tries to convince Gilgamesh to leave but Gilgamesh replies, "Two people will not perish! . . . No one can cut through a three-ply cloth!"

We should remember two things about strength.

First, we should always seek to be the strength others need, especially in their time of need. Second, we should not run into our rabbit holes when things get bad. We should, rather, call on a friend. Interesting how in the verse we see a progression from two to three. Apparently three is not a crowd.

Think about the times you have felt the most encouraged. For me, the times praying with my wife or sharing a hardship with a friend come to mind. And still other times are recalled, like when I stood surrounded by a group of people I loved. We shared, we sang, we prayed, we laughed, and I left with strength for the path ahead—moving to England.

In sports we hear about "team chemistry" and how important it is for a team to possess it. If players bond and place the needs of their teammates first, they find success. But if players isolate themselves, or act selfishly, they weaken the team.

It is also possible to be, to work, to live within a group of people and yet remain isolated. Many things put us there—things like shame, fear, selfishness, and greed, all stemming from a vision turned inward, toward the dark, toward our selves. The greatest conqueror among us, however, finds new vision in the hope of conquest, in the light of service, and in the strength of brotherhood.

Jesus said, "I call you friends." Then he went and died for us. Oh, to wrap ourselves around him—each of us, locking arms, locking hearts. Strong.

Today's Prayer

Lord Jesus, remember my loved ones in your grace today. Help me be a better friend, a better son/daughter/spouse. I want to add to the strength of those around me. But I can only do that if you are my strength.

Family Blessing   DAY 5

The command we have from Christ is blunt: Loving God includes loving people. You've got to love both.

1 John 4:21 THE MESSAGE

Take today and prepare for the "family gathering," or that thing we call church—you know, where Christians gather to worship God together. That is where the family is getting together. How can you ready yourself now to enter into the gathering ready to be a loving sister or brother?

So often we treat Sunday as a duty, a chore, a bookend to our week. What if we viewed it as a special time to see what is going on with the family—to take care of our business and do a bit of worth-giving to God? When you view church as a place to gather with family, your perspective will shift. Giving will replace getting. When that shift occurs, the gathering dynamic will change. Love will fill the halls of the building and hearts will break, will mend, will soar.

Consider your sisters and brothers even now. Pray for them as you would your own family—"Lord, how can I be a blessing to my family on Sunday?" Think of church less like an organization and more like the relational hub of your spiritual life. When you do, the shortcomings of programming will mean less to you. You will forget about your preferences in worship and youth ministry because you will be more concerned with the preference of the family.

Let us hold hands and pray, like a family around the dinner table. Let us support our family members with the brilliance of stern love and up-building joy.

Today's Prayer

Lord Jesus, I cannot control my love for my family. Help me be a blessing to them.

Kindness

I Will Join You in Weakness

> Be kind and compassionate to one another, forgiving each other,
> just as in Christ God forgave you.
>
> Ephesians 4:32 NIV

I've caught myself telling my daughters to be kind to each other as I holler at them for being unkind. How embarrassing. If you'll allow me, I'll ask a five-year-old's question and attempt to answer it: "Where does kindness come from?"

Kindness does not come from busyness, that's for certain. I think we can also rule out kindness stemming from self-centeredness.

"When do you find yourself most kind?"

I find myself most kind when I'm figuring out what someone else needs or when I'm giving of myself in some way—time, resources, insight. In the midst of being kind, I find myself evaluating my action.

Oh, this is what it is to be kind. Things are slower in this world. Things are more at ease. Why am I so hasty?

When I search my *New Oxford Dictionary*, I find *kindness* and *compassionate* to be synonyms. They express the same thing: "I will meet you where you are weakest and not judge you, but join you, hold your hand, and walk with you."

Today's Prayer

Lord Jesus, enable me to join and walk with others.

What Does Kindness Say?   DAY 2

My sacrifice, O God, is a broken spirit; a broken and contrite heart you, God, will not despise.

Psalm 51:17 NIV

Priest and writer Henri Nouwen says that in order for compassion to grow in an individual, he or she must dive into the discipline of solitude. "Compassion is the fruit of solitude and the fruit of all ministry," he says.[1]

Solitude, in our modern culture, does not come easy or without specific intention.

"In solitude," continues Nouwen, "our heart of stone can be turned into a heart of flesh, a rebellious heart into a contrite heart, and a closed heart into a heart that can open itself to all suffering people in a gesture of solidarity."[2]

When I am most stressed, I am most unkind, compassion wanes. To unlock the vault of kindness within, I must release those things that tie my mind and spirit to stress: provision issues—*Will projects keep coming?*—and procrastination and other issues I haven't given to God.

My wife and I ask each other, "What would kindness say here?" The only way we can answer that question is if we've given the situation some thought and ambled around in solitude for a spell.

Today's Prayer

*Lord Jesus, may your kindness and compassion remind me
to slow down enough to feel my fist unclench.*

A Tender Heart   DAY 3

Today's Prayer

*Lord Jesus, you tell us to be kind to others, tenderhearted,
forgiving, as you forgave us. I find this at times to be too
hard for my human heart. It wants to hold on to bitterness.
It wants to clinch while you tell me to release. Sometimes
I want to be angry—it feeds me. But a diet of anger leads
only to hell.*

*When I am unkind, I feel so far from you. I hate that
feeling, but I also struggle to reach back to you and accept
your forgiveness. I want to feed on you, the Bread of Life.
Keep hell away from me.*

Struggle, Together   DAY 4

Bear with each other and forgive one another if any of you has
a grievance against someone. Forgive as the Lord forgave you.

Colossians 3:13 NIV

I love this short exhortation from Ignatius of Antioch (he was
a late-first-century bishop of the Christian church, martyred
in 115 AD): "Labor with one another, struggle together, run
together, suffer together, rest together, rise up together as God's
stewards and assessors and servants."

When you labor with someone, you, in essence, choose to join them in their work. You get your hands dirty. You experience what they experience. You can relate to them in a more intimate way because you have calloused your hands right along with them.

Relational currency grows when you labor with someone. If you want to succeed in your labor you will learn to bear one another's grievances. You will learn to forgive quickly. Your love will grow so strong that forgiveness will be of little use because love will cover.

The apostle Paul says struggle exists as a way for us to relate to one another, to offer help to one another. Have you experienced a particular tragedy or pain? The scar may hurt from time to time, but the pain you bore can now be used to encourage another person going through the same thing.

In an increasingly fragmented world, let us allow our faith to draw us close to one another. Let us struggle, together, and learn of God's glory through the mending cracks of our toil.

Today's Prayer

Lord Jesus, give me strength to struggle well with my brothers and sisters.

He Knows   DAY 5

For we do not have a high priest who is unable to sympathize with our weaknesses, but one who in every respect has been tempted as we are, yet without sin.

Hebrews 4:15

On the days I struggle to labor with others, to walk with them, to carry their burdens, to be kind, I think of Christ.

It is, at times, the only thing that keeps me from deep melancholy. If I do not quickly run to him in prayer, I am lost.

When you blow it with your friends, when your children badger you to the point of insanity, take heart. Our God is not some distant deity. He relates, and he loves. If you are like me, you cannot fathom how deep his love runs. I shudder to think of its depth—and the thought also comforts me. For where else can I go and drown in love?

Today's Prayer

Lord Jesus, thank you for understanding. Thank you for loving me into kindness.

Gentleness

Downcast and Unrelenting   DAY 1

Why are you cast down, O my soul, and why are you in tur-
moil within me? Hope in God; for I shall again praise him, my
salvation.

Psalm 42:5

Why is it so difficult to live in the gentleness of the Holy
Spirit? Why is darkness within us such a hostile and
unrelenting force? Our patience wears thin too quickly. Our
words fly sharp at those we love. Our attitudes grind themselves
in the shadows of self-pity.

I want to "bless the Lord, O my soul." I want to "worship
your holy name."

And then we turn to the Word and find the poems of David—
like he collected them for you and me, for this moment.

"Why so downcast, O my soul?" Put your hope in God. For
hope is not far off.

What is the remedy for a hostile spirit? For me, I must first live in the awareness of myself and how my spirit affects others: my family, my friends, my co-workers, my colleagues. Then I must possess the courage to recognize the need to stop and regroup— to collect myself in quietness. I must be contrite enough for prayer to drip from my lips. Haughtiness does its best to keep me stiff-necked and stubborn, unable to pray.

Today's Prayer

Lord Jesus, give me victory over despair. Do not let it affect my attitude and the way I treat others.

Aware and Serving   DAY 2

Do not repay evil for evil or reviling for reviling, but on the contrary, bless, for to this you were called, that you may obtain a blessing.

1 Peter 3:9

If I am not stiff-necked, then I pray I am aware enough to realize I need to serve. When I serve the Lord, I find myself setting out to serve others. I must, at times, jolt myself back into a mind-set of God-first, because it is too easy to live me-first.

Serving engenders gentleness, for it is a genteel posture. I subvert my own pride, which flares into rough action, gruff talk, and coarse thinking.

Not reacting to the unkindness of others or to ill treatment from others—that alone affords life to my bones!

But before I can be gentle in my reactions and my intentions, I must first cultivate gentleness within my heart. In my heart the floods well up—and so I must protect my heart, for it is the wellspring of life. If I allow dirt and grime and muck into my heart via the media I consume (books, films, music, etc.) and the company I keep, life will not spring forth from my mouth and actions. Rather, death will reign and I will want retribution for all the wrongs done to me, even the tiniest slight.

I am finding my heart, the one from heaven, and it sparkles.

Today's Prayer

Lord Jesus, I want to be gentle, and I need your strength to kill the brute within so that heaven can live where darkness easily presides.

Grace in Your Law   DAY 3

Today's Prayer

Lord Jesus, your law is perfect, reviving the soul;
your testimony is sure, making wise the simple;
your precepts are right, rejoicing the heart;
your commandment is pure, enlightening the eyes;
the fear of you, O Lord, is clean, enduring forever;
your rules are true, and righteous altogether.
                            —adapted from Psalm 19:7–9

My Strength Is No Strength   DAY 4

But the fruit of the Spirit is love, joy, peace, patience, kindness, goodness, faithfulness, gentleness, self-control; against such things there is no law.

Galatians 5:22

I can be about as patient as a two-year-old wanting more Cheerios at breakfast. Patience is a virtue that, for me, comes only after much practice and copious amounts of prayer. And even then, it's only the Holy Spirit's work within these dry, impatient bones.

There are times when I lose all patience, and my reaction to a situation spirals into self-serving anger. It's during those moments that I wonder if the Spirit really has any power over the old me at all. For, at base, I am a creature of force.

In Paul's letter to the Galatians, he emphasizes true Christian freedom because the Galatians fell under a false interpretation of it. After being duped into a lifestyle of law-keeping, emphasizing works of the flesh, the Galatians ironically fell into a self-serving immorality.

Our efforts to please God in our own strength result only in sinful behavior. The Galatians experienced this firsthand. Their sinful behavior festered in their personal relationships. They lived in danger of devouring one another through their biting and loveless interactions.

We think the law is so bad. *By God, we want our Christian freedom, and now!* But the law is less a list of dos and don'ts and more of a "way." John the Beloved ate with, talked with, and lived with the Way. For it is Christ himself.

"I am *the Way!*" says Jesus.

Today's Prayer
Lord Jesus, keep me from devouring those whom I love, and help me to walk in the Way.

Hell Pursuing, Spirit Living   DAY 5

But if you have bitter jealousy and selfish ambition in your hearts, do not boast and be false to the truth. This is not the wisdom that comes down from above, but is earthly, unspiritual, demonic. For where jealousy and selfish ambition exist, there will be disorder and every vile practice.

James 3:14–16

When we fail to walk in the Way, we tend to walk another path—a path we think will lead to the good life. But that way crumbles into selfish immorality. Our self-producing godliness deceives us—we sleep our holiness away in the arms of other people, we destroy one another with our words, and we trample each other under the force of our stride as we walk down the way of hell itself.

I feel hell biting at my heels when I act out of my impatience—it's like the Spirit evaporates from the room, replaced by the stench of a wayward morality.

Am I making too much of our relationships? I don't think so. How we treat one another is how we treat the rest of the world, a world searching for the Way. Our relationships form our families, form our friendship circles, form our communities, and form our work environments. It all starts with how we treat our siblings and parents, our spouses and children, and our friends.

Today's Prayer

Lord Jesus, I want to walk in you, for you are the Way. Help me stride with you as your Spirit works in me—producing life-giving fruit, rising from my ashes and blooming into patience.

Faithfulness

Belief

Blessed are those who have not seen and yet have believed.

John 20:29

Do I believe in you, God, one time, and that's it? I confess I believe, and I do, but today I don't—at least I don't feel like I believe. Is that the same as not believing? Because I always return to you.

I want to live like I believe all the time. But some days everything I see, these trees, this sky, this grass, they all look void, though they remain unchanged since yesterday. Can you reach me here in this despondency?

Some days a simple physical meeting would do wonders. Can't you meet me here next to my bookcases and desk? Should we meet down on the deck before anyone rises, before the mayhem of the morning overtakes? Then I could walk through the day with a knowing grin—no one would know I saw you, just me. And the trees, sky, and grass would regain their color.

Why isn't every day filled with the feeling of your presence, even though I know it is? My belief only grows the more I seek you. But some days I grow weary of seeking. I want all these things added unto me, but I'm tired of the pursuit. Can you wait for me?

I'm trapped in this place, this world where the cynic rules and ignorance guised in the sophistication of doubt makes belief unfashionable. And yet I recall the rules of belief. If I say I believe, then I must follow. I must trudge through this weak despondency—writing myself through it just to keep pace with you.

Bonhoeffer said, "Only he who believes is obedient, and only he who is obedient believes."[1] My obedience does not see the colorless sky and opaque trees. It only sees you, God. I obey even when I can't see, and then find myself back in belief. Belief, that blind guide into eternity.

Today's Prayer
Lord Jesus, help my belief today. Strengthen my obedience.

When All You Do Is Not Enough   DAY 2

I have chosen the way of faithfulness; I set your rules before me.

Psalm 119:30

What else can I do? I've put in the time. I've done my duty. I've fulfilled my obligations. And still it's not enough. Why does God tease me with dreams, when they dissolve with ease and without care to my heart?

Even though I doubt, I still persevere. And for what? For character? What will that get me?

Still, I return to my first love, over and over—its resonance shaking me within and without. But though I love, I do not overcome.

The straight is so narrow, I lose my balance. But the path seems to end—weeds and thistles reach into the path and cut. Where does this path lead anyway?

How can Habakkuk speak these words? "Though the fig tree does not bud, and there are no grapes on the vines . . . yet I will rejoice in the Lord" (3:17–18 NIV).

My heart is no God target; he does not pull his bow to unleash his hot arrows upon me. I do not lift up idols. I am not running from my task. Why, then, the travail?

And yet my heart knows nothing else but the fierceness of his love. I walk. I run. I bound up the mountain set before me. I fall back to the place where I began. Broken bones, broken spirit, I sit in a heap.

The wind blows my name and pushes me back to the mountain's side. "Climb," it says. "Climb, my son."

The dead-end path of narrow thistles landed me here, in front of this mountain. And a Spirit wind speaks to me.

"We are not responsible for success," writes theologian Klaus Bockmuehl, "but we remain responsible for obedience."[2]

And so, we climb.

Today's Prayer

Lord Jesus, be my "enough" today.

Valley of Duty   DAY 3

Today's Prayer

Lord Jesus, what does it look like to be faithful? For too long I labored in this valley of duty. But faithfulness does not look like the dutiful son or daughter. It looks like love. You remain faithful because you love me—indeed you are love itself! And love does not fail. Obedience, faithfulness—both grow out of love.

So when I act, when I do, when I show love, when I help others, when I sing praise, I am doing it not from some forceful heavenly hand. I am doing it because I cannot help myself. Since you—the very essence of love!—reside within me, I live and breathe and do, love.

Surge from me today, Lord Jesus. May your love overwhelm me that I may do likewise to the world, through my faithfulness, through my obedience.

A Faithful Life   DAY 4

For we walk by faith, not by sight.

2 Corinthians 5:7

Because love forms our faithfulness and obedience, we can live a life of faith without fear. This translates into our everydays in great ways. If we are faithful, if we obey the voice of Christ in our lives, we will do as he prompts.

What does that look like?

For me, it looks like the shaky hand of my wife pushing the purchase button, buying five one-way tickets for our family to move to England. We both knew, beyond a shadow of doubt, God was pointing us toward England. Everything was aligned, we just needed to act. Buy the tickets! We did, and we did not combust. The obedient act drew us even closer to God. "Yes, God, I see how you supported and provided when we did what you told us to do. Now, what's next?"

Today's Prayer

Lord Jesus, I feel you prompting me. I am afraid. Help me to live faithfully. I am ready to act.

I AM   DAY 5

Jesus Christ is the same yesterday and today and forever.

Hebrews 13:8

*A*n adaptation from the Gospel of John and 1 Corinthians 1 . . .

In the beginning was the Word. The Word was with God. The Word was God. That was *me*. I was the Word and still am the Word. All things were made through me—and without me, nothing would have been made.

Do you believe this?

In me was life—I teem with it. And that life was the light of men. And that light shines in the darkness. And the darkness will never overcome it. Do you believe *this*?

But then I came to you in order to draw you back to the Father—to make a way for everyone to be in our family. I came walking among you, performing signs and wonders. Some believed. Others did not. Some believed for a short while. But when they found out that I was not the one they expected, they shouted for my death.

Who do you expect me to be? Do you not know that . . .

I am the Bread of Life. The person who aligns with me hungers no more and thirsts no more, *ever*. I have told you this explicitly because even though you have seen me in action, you don't really believe me. Do you?

I am the world's Light. No one who follows me stumbles around in the darkness. I provide plenty of light to live in. Can you see? Are you stumbling?

I tell you the truth; I am the gate for the sheep. All who came before me were thieves and robbers. But the true sheep did not listen to them. Yes, I am the gate. Those who come in through me will be saved. Indeed, I am the good shepherd. And the good shepherd sacrifices his life for the sheep. Don't you want to be rescued?

I am the resurrection and the life. Anyone who believes in me will live, even after dying. Can you not see that I *am* the Way and the Truth and the Life? No one comes to the Father except through me.

I am the true vine, and my Father is the vinedresser. Every branch in me that does not bear fruit he takes away, and every branch that does bear fruit he prunes, that it may bear more fruit. I want to see you bloom—you delight me so.

But I realize the message of my cross is foolish to those who are headed for destruction!

So where does this leave the philosophers, the scholars, and the world's brilliant debaters? My Father has made the wisdom of this world look foolish. He has, in his wisdom, seen to it that the world would never know him through human wisdom; he has used your foolish preaching to save those who *believe*. That's how he works. Don't you realize this?

It is foolish to the Jews, who ask for signs from heaven. And it is foolish to the Greeks, who seek human wisdom. Are you like one of them? Looking to and fro for a sign, thinking your intelligence will save you?

Come to me, if you are weak and heavy laden, and you will find rest for your souls. For I AM your Lord and Adonai; YHWH, the preexisting One. I come that you might *believe*.

Today's Prayer

Lord Jesus, I will be faithful, because I believe in you—the I AM.

Leadership

Looking for Direction

Clothe yourselves, all of you, with humility toward one another, for "God opposes the proud but gives grace to the humble."

1 Peter 5:5

The world is watching. Certainly times arise when we should care less about what people think. But as Christians bearing the banner of Christ Jesus, you and I live as ambassadors. Too often we cop out and say, "But I'm not a leader. Who really cares what I do?"

Let us not be shortsighted and selfish. Whether you lead a bank as its CEO or you grow your family with your spouse, you lead. The outside world is watching, and people want to know why they should care about Jesus. Your actions, your beliefs, and how you communicate those beliefs matter. The gospel will spread because you and I will lead our communities to Christ by the veracity and sincerity of our rhetoric backed by a way of life that mirrors the passion of our hearts.

"Let us overcome by our manner of living," writes early church father John Chrysostom, "rather than by our words alone. For this is the main battle, this is the unanswerable argument, the argument from conduct."[1] Jesus left us as ambassadors to his way. It is a way uncommon in a withering world. So every follower of Jesus is, in a very real sense, a leader. We're commissioned with a sacred task, to make disciples and to baptize them into the family of God.

Christians, however, find we must debate the best way in which to carry out this task. Some say tell the world, others say show the world. But we must do both. Let us seek leadership in the public square and at our dinner tables, and let us do it in a way that points the world and our friends and families to Christ.

Today's Prayer

Lord Jesus, I want to lead those I love and connect with, including myself, in a way that glorifies you—through humility, through eager passion, and through a lifestyle that matches the strength of my beliefs.

Freedom From the Inner Ring   DAY 2

Live as people who are free, not using your freedom as a cover-up for evil, but living as servants of God.

1 Peter 2:16

You and I cannot escape the pull toward self-promotion. It invades each day through various mediums. And the very culture that tells us to hoist up our personal banners everywhere is the same culture that empowers us to act as our own judge and jury. It tells us that permissive behavior is the norm.

Though we cannot escape the cultural pull, we need not give in to it.

We must recover the lost art of reflection. If we wait and reflect instead of reacting to situations, people, and "news," we should find a most helpful friend: *discernment*. This friend draws a hard line, one our pride finds stark and uninviting.

Today, as we ready our hearts and minds for the day's interactions, let us consider how we might join the practice of quiet reflection with true Christian freedom.

They seem opposed: restraining from reaction yet exercising freedom. But they are, in fact, kindred.

The apostle Peter reminds his readers, "Live as people who are free, not using your freedom as a cover-up for evil, but living as servants of God. Honor everyone. Love the brotherhood. Fear God. Honor the emperor" (1 Peter 2:16–17).

Christian freedom means we are free to follow God's will. We are, like Paul, slaves to the gospel. As such, we do not live as permissive agents of cheap grace and license. Rather, we adhere to a specific code: Every person is to be shown respect, our Christian brothers and sisters are to be loved, God is to be approached in reverent fear, and our authorities are to be respected.

Today's Prayer

Lord Jesus, teach me to be discerning in all my daily interactions.

Springs of Life   DAY 3

Today's Prayer

Lord Jesus, help me to keep my heart with all vigilance, for from it flows the springs of life. I want to put away crooked speech from my lips, as well as devious talk. I seek to set my gaze directly forward so that I can see all that is before me with eyes of wisdom. Help me to discern my path so that my way will be sure, and I will prosper in your sight. Keep me from turning to the right or to the left; keep me away from evil.[2]

Actions Reveal Motives   DAY 4

For am I now seeking the approval of man, or of God? Or am I trying to please man? If I were still trying to please man, I would not be a servant of Christ.

Galatians 1:10

It's easy to forget what could be called the Christian code: to show every person respect, to love our Christian brothers and sisters, to approach God in reverent fear, and to respect our authorities. In the pursuit to build a leadership platform, influence, and a personal brand, or secure a raise or a position, we pounce on opportunity.

I often see this in the world of blogs and writing. In the name of "being prophetic," or "holding some Christian leader accountable," or "just because I can," writers and talking heads wield their words as battle-axes. They scramble to be heard and seen and, of course, followed. At some level, all of us desire to exist and be seen as a person of the inner circle of our chosen professions.

But why?

In his address titled "The Inner Ring," C. S. Lewis warns against the pursuit of the "in" crowd. Such a pursuit often demands character compromises. Because we desire exclusivity, to be in the know, to be deemed as cool, to be accepted, or to be viewed as exceptional, we disregard our Christian code. We offer convenient excuses for our selfish actions.

Lewis counters this mind-set with the challenge to break the inner ring. By not pursuing it, you and I strip it of its powers. If we stick to our own work, our own endeavors, then we will find ourselves in the middle of something quite special. "You will be one of the sound craftsmen," says Lewis, "and other sound craftsmen will know it."[3] By focusing on your own craft, you become one of the ones whom people on the outside of your profession want to know.

If we set out each day to work, to hone our craft—whatever it may be—then we create a culture that cares little for the pull of self-promotion and permissive behavior. We create a safe place where respect and love and reverence flourish.

The same idea goes for the people you associate with outside of your craft—the times you gather with friends. Lewis says:

> And if in your spare time you consort simply with the people you like, you will again find that you have come unawares to a real inside, that you are indeed snug and safe at the centre of something which, seen from without, would look exactly like an Inner Ring.[4]

Lewis practiced what he preached. That is why whole books have been written about his own "inner ring" known as the Inklings—a diverse group of friends who met together, enjoyed one another, challenged one another, and cared not for what the popular crowd thought or did.

The wisdom here is simple: Do what you love, and do it well. Be with the people you care the most for, and care for them well. And if you do, you will find yourself caring less for the inner ring and more for those we should be caring for anyway: our true friends.

Today's Prayer

Lord, grow us in your patience. Strengthen us as we strive to live in the freedom of your Way.

Leadership That Flourishes DAY 5

Anyone who intends to come with me has to let me lead. You're not in the driver's seat; I am. Don't run from suffering; embrace it. Follow me and I'll show you how. Self-help is no help at all. Self-sacrifice is the way, my way, to finding yourself, your true self. What kind of deal is it to get everything you want but lose yourself? What could you ever trade your soul for?

Matthew 16:24–26 THE MESSAGE

The flourishing leader looks like a man or woman following Jesus with passion and intent. Henri Nouwen says mature leaders are willing "to be led where they would rather not go."

To follow Jesus to his cross demands a deep spiritual affection— you and I must love Jesus so much that we'd go anywhere with him and for him. Some think this kind of leadership weak. But that is not the case.

Jesus does not call us to roll over or be spineless. But he does call us to a place of powerlessness. "It is not a leadership of power and control," writes Nouwen about Christian leadership, "but a leadership of powerlessness and humility, in which the suffering servant of God, Jesus Christ, is made manifest."[5]

The humble leader understands and lives by the truth: truth of self, truth of others, and the truth of their situation. The powerless leader abandons power in favor of love.

This is the person whose leadership knows no bounds, the leader who is led by Christ. Do you know this kind of leader?

Are you this kind of leader? In your home? In your friendships? In your school? In your business? In your church?

You spot leaders who lead for their own gain, the ones bent on self-help, power, and control. They're the ones vying for the limelight and the accolades.

Who among us will lead the church and our families and our businesses into the future? It is the leader, as Nouwen says, who can be led.

"I AM the Way . . ." And so Christ is. May we *follow* him as we *walk in* him.

Today's Prayer

Lord Jesus, lead me in your Way. I want to be led by you so that I can lead others, so that I can serve others.

The Long Pause

The Long Pause" is here to remind you to take a break from the normal routine and reflect, not only on this longer piece, but also on your own life rhythms. What needs to change? What needs to stop? What do you need more of? Use this long-form piece, along with the reflection questions, as something to contemplate throughout the week.

God of the Ridiculous

To be a Christian means to believe in the ridiculous. Of course, one who *is* a Christian does not see belief like this. Christians view the ridiculous as normalcy, and, in turn, the world views them with contempt for their sheer lunacy.

Abraham, that champion of faith, was chief of the ridiculous lunatics.

> . . . he stood there, the old man with his only hope! But he did not doubt, he did not look in anguish to the left or right, he did not challenge heaven with his prayers. He knew it was God the Almighty that tried him, he knew it was the hardest

sacrifice that could be demanded of him; but he also knew that no sacrifice was too hard when God demanded it—and he drew his knife.[1]

We stand daily in the light of certain ridiculousness—a paradoxical combination of certitude and unknowing. The writer of Hebrews spells it out for us.

> The fundamental fact of existence is that this trust in God, this faith, is the firm foundation under everything that makes life worth living. It's our handle on what we can't see.
>
> Hebrews 11:1 THE MESSAGE

As one on the inside of ridiculousness, I view belief and faith in the same light. The world, however, views belief as separate from faith. Faith to the world is radical adherence to religious dogma, and belief is that aspect of faith that moves a person from onlooker to participant. The world views the holding of beliefs as helpful, but not as true.

How do you view belief? Faith? Do you live daily like Abraham, drawing your knife?

Our daily vision for work and life will either soar or flail depending on the veracity of our belief. Do you live like it is true, or is it merely helpful—a crutch to get you through the muck of life? Once you and I pass over into the land of belief, action predicated on doubt is no longer an option. "Abraham had faith and did not doubt. He believed the ridiculous."[2]

Reflection

1. Take a few moments this week to write down your thoughts about your personal faith. Ask yourself if, when life gets sticky with unpredictability, you trust Jesus with your heart and actions as much as your words express.

2. Do you think every Christian is called to live like Abraham? Some people think only great spiritual leaders live like that, but then why does God include it in his Word to us?

3. Should your life look a bit more ridiculous? I do not mean ridiculous in the idiotic sense, but in the sense that when your name comes up, the first thing people comment on is your robust faith.

4. Some philosophers regard the Christian faith as explainable right up to the resurrection. After that, only faith explains it, and only a person of faith can grasp it. How deeply does the resurrection affect your everyday attitude, decisions, and passions?

Application

1. Have you made any promises to God in recent months? Do you feel guilty for not following through, if that's the case? Or have you found a new sense of blessing or victory due to exercising your faith?

2. If you have faltered in your goals with God, wipe the slate clean and begin fresh this week. Evaluate the depth of your faith, your response to struggle over the past several months, and give it all back to Christ.

3. If, during the previous "Long Pause," you began a journal, then revisit that week and pray through your reflections since then. Discuss your progress with a friend or loved one. This should be a regular occurrence for you throughout the year. I'm constantly taking my wife out to discuss God's direction in our lives. It helps me see where God has taken me, how he's strengthened my personal faith, and where he's directing me next.

4. I believe giving monetarily is a good barometer of my faith. Everything I say I believe becomes very real when a check is written. I'm not suggesting a legalistic accounting of your tithing. Rather, I'm asking you to consider how real

your trust in the Lord is by looking at how you actually apply your faith. I've had friends tell me they struggle with Sabbath rest because when they're honest with themselves, they struggle with trusting God with their money. They must work to feel provided for. This week, pray about your giving and reflect on where your treasure lies—for there you will find your trust.

Prayer

Hallowed Be

Pray, then, in this way. . . .

Matthew 6:9 NASB

W hen you pray, do so with your heart pointed at God. That is all you need to remember. In Matthew's Gospel, Jesus gives his famous Lord's Prayer as a summary. He's not offering us a prescribed ritual kind of prayer. Rather, he's giving us direction for our own prayers, for our own heart, soul, and mind pointed toward God. His prayer, then, is our model.

When you forget your heart and cannot find the words to pray, use the words of Jesus. Even more, use his model: *reverence* and *ascribed worth*, *submission* to and *anticipation* of God's will, thanksgiving and total reliance upon him, confession, petition (ask God for his help), and for leading and guidance.

We pray not to fulfill religious practice, but to talk with God and listen to him. Use words when you pray, but also use silence. What does your heart hear?

Our Father who is in heaven,
Hallowed be Your name.
Your kingdom come.
Your will be done,
On earth as it is in heaven.
Give us this day our daily bread.
And forgive us our debts, as we also have forgiven our
    debtors.
And do not lead us into temptation, but deliver us from
    evil. For Yours is the kingdom and the power and the
    glory forever. Amen.

Matthew 6:9–13 NASB

Today's Prayer

Lord Jesus, show me how to pray. No frills, no big words, just me in the rawness of this life. And yet, even in my rawness I want to honor and glorify you. I want to approach you with the reverence you deserve.

Puritan Prayer   DAY 2

Every morning
you'll hear me at it again.
Every morning
I lay out the pieces of my life
on your altar
and watch for fire to descend.

Psalm 5:3 THE MESSAGE

Are you at it again as well, laying out the pieces of your life? Some days are heavier than others. The pieces collect and weigh us down. Today, don't let the pieces weigh you down. Get up and pray a strong prayer.

Today's Prayer

Lord Jesus, the author of all good, I come to thee for the grace another day will require for its duties and events. I step out into a wicked world; I carry about with me an evil heart. I know that without thee I can do nothing—that everything with which I shall be concerned, however harmless in itself, may prove an occasion of sin or folly, unless I am kept by thy power. Hold me up and I shall be safe.

Preserve my understanding from subtlety of error, my affections from love of idols, my character from stain of vice, my profession from every form of evil. May I engage in nothing in which I cannot implore thy blessing, and in which I cannot invite thy inspection. Prosper me in all lawful undertakings, or prepare me for disappointments. Give me neither poverty nor riches. Feed me with food convenient for me, lest I be full and deny thee and say, Who is the Lord? or be poor, and steal, and take thy name in vain.

May every creature be made good to me by prayer and thy will. Teach me how to use the world and not abuse it, to improve my talents, to redeem my time, to walk in wisdom toward those without and in kindness to those within, to do good to all men and especially to my fellow Christians. And to thee be the glory.[1]

Moans of the Spirit   DAY 3

Today's Prayer

Lord Jesus, I pray you, of great goodness, would make known to me, and take from my heart, every kind and form and degree of pride, whether it be from evil spirits or my own corrupt nature; and that you would awaken in me the deepest depth and truth of that humility, which can make me capable of your light and Holy Spirit.[2]

I take comfort in your Word, for "the Spirit helps us in our weakness. For we do not know what to pray for as we ought, but the Spirit himself intercedes for us with groanings too deep for words. And he who searches hearts knows what is the mind of the Spirit, because the Spirit intercedes for the saints according to the will of God" (Romans 8:26–27).

The Apostles' Creed   DAY 4

Jesus said to him, "Thomas, because you have seen Me, you have believed. Blessed are those who have not seen and yet have believed."

John 20:29 NKJV

Use daily prayer, your breathing-prayer, to strengthen your faith. Remind yourself through and during prayer who God is, who his Son is, and what he did for you. What is it you believe?

I believe in God the Father Almighty, Maker of heaven and earth. And in Jesus Christ, his only begotten Son, our Lord.

Who is Jesus? Who is he to you?

Jesus was conceived by the Holy Ghost, born of the Virgin Mary.

And what did he do for you?

Suffered under Pontius Pilate; was crucified, dead, and buried: He descended into hell. The third day he rose again from the dead. He ascended into heaven, and sits at the right hand of God the Father Almighty. From thence he shall come to judge the quick and the dead.

And whom has Jesus given to you and me as comfort? Do you believe?

I believe in the Holy Ghost.

And what of this gathering of people called the church? Do you bicker and argue with those in the church? Do you quibble about things that make no difference in the fundamentals of the faith? What do you believe?

I believe in the holy catholic church: the communion of saints. The forgiveness of sins.

And what of this life? What of the next life? Remind yourself today. What do you believe?

The resurrection of the body, and the life everlasting.

Today's Prayer

Lord Jesus, refresh my belief today. Renew my spiritual vision so that I can see you once more through the eyes of innocent faith. I believe, and I know why I believe, and this comforts me.

Moving God   DAY 5

Never stop praying.
1 Thessalonians 5:17 NLT

We pray, or at least we should, because we cannot help it. It should be like breathing. Paul tells us to pray without ceasing. But in order to accomplish unceasing prayer, we must have an unrelenting faith. The Christian appears to the world as a sort of maniac, spewing little whispers here and there to the Unseen. But faith says, "So be it. I believe it, and therefore, I continue to talk to the sky not because I am mad, but because

I will go mad if I cease to search for the Unseen." E. M. Bounds says of prayer:

> In the ultimate issue, prayer is simply faith, claiming its natural yet marvelous prerogatives—faith taking possession of its illimitable inheritance. True godliness is just as true, steady, and persevering in the realm of faith as it is in the province of prayer. Moreover: when faith ceases to pray, it ceases to live. Faith does the impossible because it brings God to undertake for us, and nothing is impossible with God.[3]

For our faith to remain vibrant, we must breathe prayer. We must speak to God about everything. Do you find yourself adrift today? This week? This year? How is your prayer life? If you stop talking to your friends or your spouse, what will happen? The relationship will deteriorate. Communication gives life to relationships, and the same is true with our relationship with God.

But prayer is not to be an "I need, I need, I need" type of one-way discourse. Rather, we should pray to move things—to move ourselves closer to God, to move others toward him, to invade reality with the One who can change it. To finish today's reflection, consider further the words of E. M. Bounds on moving God with prayer:

> Prayer projects faith on God, and God on the world. Only God can move mountains, but faith and prayer move God. In His cursing of the fig-tree our Lord demonstrated His power. Following that, He proceeded to declare, that large powers were committed to faith and prayer, not in order to kill but to make alive, not to blast but to bless.[4]

Today's Prayer

Lord Jesus, thank you for prayer—for a way to talk to you about my most intimate needs and desires, for a way to know you deeper each day.

Holy

Experiencing the Holy

> For you alone are holy.
> Revelation 15:4

God is the great paradox. He is the Great Magnificence, and yet in Christ we find the servant of all. He whispers worlds into existence, and cries out for help on a cross.

The nineteenth-century theologian Rudolf Otto described this awful goodness as *numinous*. He uses the term to describe that extra something attached to the term *holy*. We know that holiness implies a certain amount of moral goodness. But who among us has not experienced something more when worshiping God? Is God-worship simply admitting to God his own moral goodness? That is certainly part of it. But Otto suggests there is a kind of dread to holiness.

Have you experienced a kind of gasping during worship and prayer? Have you ever sung a song in church and tears fell down your face and you did not know why exactly, only that it felt right and good and sad and wonderful and dreadful? That is the part of holiness Otto is getting at.

If you have read (or even seen) *The Lion, the Witch and the Wardrobe*, you have encountered this holy dread. Lucy wanted to know if Aslan was safe, to which Mr. Beaver answered, "Of course he isn't safe. But he's good." That is the *numinous*—a holy quality that is at once alluring and outside yourself, as well as striking a bit of fear into you.

In *The Problem of Pain*, C. S. Lewis describes it as the feeling you would experience if someone told you that a spirit was waiting for you in the other room. Reality quakes, for there is something very terrible and possibly very good waiting for you. It is the dread you experience when you encounter something totally "other."

But perhaps you cannot relate to what I am describing. Otto confronts such readers in his book and tells them to read no further. But on this first day of the week, we shall not turn back. Rather, we shall pray.

Today's Prayer

Lord Jesus, help me to experience the fullness of your holiness.

The Beautiful Tremendous   DAY 2

For Christ has entered, not into holy places made with hands, which are copies of the true things, but into heaven itself, now to appear in the presence of God on our behalf.

Hebrews 9:24

The storm rolls in, tremendous and vast. The darkness it brings, the heaving it triggers, all quakes before the storm. And yet I cannot look away. I cannot pull my heart from the vision before me. Its flashes and rumblings—fierce, mysterious, beautiful.

God, my Storm, is mysterious and striking. I am compelled to move forward by his goodness, and am frightened to do so by his *mysterium tremendum* (a mysterious and good fear).

Where has Christ gone? Into the presence of my Storm, a place unmade, a place eternal and "other."

My Storm rolls in, beautiful. It lures me beneath its darkness, which I find is not darkness at all; only openness—a sky forever rising.

Today's Prayer
Lord Jesus, rain on me. Overwhelm me.

Caught in Your Fascination   DAY 3

Today's Prayer
Lord Jesus, you fascinate me. My Storm, you are also my blue sky. I turn upside down and walk in your endlessness. I am falling forever into you. You are "other" than me and all the pain around me. You are tremendous, overwhelming my soul. You are fascinating—letting me walk in your upside-down heaven. I am caught in your fascination, O Lord, my Storm.

In Your Wake   DAY 4

"For my thoughts are not your thoughts, neither are your ways my ways," declares the Lord. "As the heavens are higher than the earth, so are my ways higher than your ways and my thoughts than your thoughts."

Isaiah 55:8–9 NIV

L ord, give us tears and remembrance of death.[1] We are undone in your wake:

> The Mighty One, God the Lord,
>> speaks and summons the earth
>> from the rising of the sun to its setting.
> Out of Zion, the perfection of beauty,
>> God shines forth.
> Our God comes; he does not keep silence;
>> before him is a devouring fire,
>> around him a mighty tempest.
> He calls to the heavens above
>> and to the earth, that he may judge his people:
> "Gather to me my faithful ones,
>> who made a covenant with me by sacrifice!"
> The heavens declare his righteousness,
>> for God himself is judge! *Selah*
>
> Psalm 50:1–6

Today's Prayer

Lord Jesus, you are holy. You are altogether other. Today I stand behind you, allowing the wake of your holiness to pass over me because I long for you and everything that goes along with you—your beauty, your massiveness, your consuming nature. I worship you today, Lord. I give you the glory you deserve.

My Story, My Terror   DAY 5

> Are you listening, dear people? I'm getting ready to speak. . . .
>
> Psalm 50:7 THE MESSAGE

D o not think the Lord is no storm. He is, and like a storm, he brings the beautiful terror of holiness into your very being. Can you hear him? He speaks, to me, to you

> Offer to God a sacrifice of thanksgiving,
>> and perform your vows to the Most High,
> and call upon me in the day of trouble;
>> I will deliver you, and you shall glorify me.
> Mark this, then, you who forget God,
>> lest I tear you apart, and there be none to deliver!
> The one who offers thanksgiving as his sacrifice glorifies me;
>> to one who orders his way rightly
> I will show the salvation of God!
>
> Psalm 50:14–15, 22–23

Today's Prayer

Lord Jesus, I hear you and seek to listen, to obey your Word. Help me to stand in your presence, slow to speak, quick to be thankful. Strengthen my faith so that I can endure your storm, your beauty, your glory.

Romance

His Gentle, Poetic Way

> Let the field exult, and everything in it! Then shall all the trees of the forest sing for joy before the Lord. . . .
>
> Psalm 96:12–13

Last Friday I absconded with my wife to a quiet wooded haven in the Georgia wild. We talked and ate and let time slip by without a fight.

Too often I hurry into tomorrow with my list and agenda. My determination wards off the now, and it slips away. But lately I've taken more time to watch the white drapes drift in the wind; I've planted more flowers; I've read more for me.

The poetry of life can't be read. It is experienced in each moment God gives to us. The prose of life makes more sense to us, though. It tells us what to do, though without color and holy ambiguity.

We cannot live life on a strict prose diet. We must venture into the wild for some poetry. We must walk with our loved ones without saying a word, just holding hands. We must play with our children, bubbling and laughing with them. We must steal the mornings away and listen to the Holy Spirit, and walk in and among his splendor—his strong and beautiful sanctuary.

Today's Prayer

Lord Jesus, give us the moments today that will last in our memories; bless them and keep them ever before us as reminders of your gentle and poetic way. Strengthen us to walk in and among your lines and stanzas and meter.

Our Inordinate Love   DAY 2

Do you think anyone is going to be able to drive a wedge between us and Christ's love for us? There is no way! Not trouble, not hard times, not hatred, not hunger, not homelessness, not bullying threats, not backstabbing, not even the worst sins listed in Scripture. . . . None of this fazes us because Jesus loves us.

Romans 8:38–39 THE MESSAGE

Here is one of C. S. Lewis's most quoted passages, for obvious reasons:

To love at all is to be vulnerable. Love anything and your heart will be wrung and possibly broken. If you want to make sure of keeping intact you must give it to no one, not even an animal. Wrap it up carefully round with hobbies and little luxuries; avoid all entanglements. Lock it up safe in the casket or coffin of your selfishness. But in that casket, safe, dark, motionless, airless, it will change. It will not be broken; it will become unbreakable, impenetrable, irredeemable. To love is to be vulnerable.[1]

Lewis is working out a thoughtful reaction to a passage in St. Augustine's *Confessions*. Augustine, who had just lost a dear friend, writes: "Though left alone, he loses none dear to him; for all are dear in the one who cannot be lost" (Book IV; xiv). Basically, to use Lewis's paraphrase, "Do not let your happiness depend on something you may lose."

Lewis says that to love at all is to hurt, to lose, and to experience pain. The alternative is to turn to stone. Lewis, unlike Augustine, is not discouraging inordinate human love but making a comment about the smallness of our love for God. "It is the smallness of our love for God, not the greatness of our love for the man, that constitutes the inordinacy."

A great passage indeed. Basically, love, and love hard. If you don't love, you'll turn to stone. It's not that we love humans too much, but that we love God not great enough.

Today's Prayer

Lord Jesus, there is a sure price to pay for loving people. We betray, we lie, and we die. And yet we continue to love, our pain in loss magnified by the amount that we love. But I must confess, today my love for you is not so great. Quite possibly, I've turned into a spiritual stone. Awaken me, Lord Jesus!

My Affections   DAY 3

Today's Prayer

Lord Jesus, I know the criteria of affection. Two objects within the bonds of affection must be familiar.[2] So for me to have strong affection for you, I must be familiar with you. How often do I wake feeling familiarity with you or the things of heaven, and yet you're new to me every morning. When my affection, when my familiarity with you wanes, you still love me.

Our First Love   DAY 4

But I have this against you, that you have abandoned the love you had at first.

Revelation 2:4

We don't always think of the Christian life as being a life of romance. But that would be a tragic mistake. Romance is not only for poets, musicians, and artists. Romance exists in us all.

Think about how your affections begin with an object. You view it and are captivated by its beauty. The beauty of the thing, however, goes further, deeper, than mere visual stimulation. The object moves you in some way within. In many ways, our affinities begin with beauty of a certain kind and stir us in such a way as to evoke a permanent affection. A dog, a song, a book, a person—all begin with a stimulus, and then over time we discover how deeply we love Bach, or Scottie the terrier, or Sarah.

This ongoing affection is romance, and it revolves around an experience. That experience of being with or near the object of our affections affects the way we live and with whom we associate and that with which we fill our imaginations.

And what of our romance with God? Where does that begin? How do we arrange our lifestyle around our affections for God? Are we in love with Jesus? Is there any romance of which to speak?

In the above verse, the writer John delivers a message to the church at Ephesus. Though they displayed great virtue in some areas, they had forsaken their first love. But is this saying they fell out of romance with God? The Ephesian church held to good doctrine but lost their love for people. Good doctrine without love for people is worthless. When we, as Christians, begin to hate the evildoers rather than the evil itself, we cease to love, and the gospel falls to perversion.

Romance with God, on the other hand, should display itself in love for other people. Had they fallen in their love for God? In a way, yes, because they failed to love people. They go hand in glove.

Today's Prayer

Lord Jesus, I admit to you, my affections for you have slipped away though ever so slowly. Restore to me the joy of my salvation—restore to me the affections of my first love, that I might love others as you have loved me. And when I have loved others, I know that my love for you will glow once more.

Beauty Will Save the World   DAY 5

> Behold, you are beautiful, my love; behold, you are beautiful.
>
> Song of Solomon 1:15

Today's reflection title is from Fyodor Dostoyevsky's novel *The Idiot*. The phrase "beauty will save the world" is part of a response during a conversation between two travelers on a train. Is it a naïve statement? Can beauty actually save anything?

I think it can. Beauty is, many times, a beginning point—it can be the impetus for love. In the case of God, we love God because he is beautiful. And how do we know he is beautiful?

Because we can see his creative masterpiece, the earth, as it encompasses us. We marvel at the sunrise and sunset. We gape at the northern lights when they sometimes dip down through a clear, cool autumn sky in North America. We stand amazed at the mountains.

How do these objects of beauty save us? Because they point somewhere else—to the beyond. If there is beauty so astounding, does it not follow that there is, perchance, a beauty giver?

You are reading this book, this entry, because you believe (at least I assume) that a beauty giver does exist. If this is the case, then this beauty giver reveals himself through the surrounding glory. Our affection, or romance, with this beauty giver matters

Beauty saves the world because people like you and me point to it. We have experienced the beauty of the landscape but found it not to end when the light passes from a sunset. Rather, we have followed the sunset to the person of Christ and found the illuminating qualities in the radiant heavens to be consistent with our understanding of who Christ is: beautiful, colorful, iridescent, faithful, soft, inviting, constant.

Today's Prayer

Lord Jesus, I want to point others to you today. I want them to see your beauty, not just in the landscape but in me. I want them to see my affection for you and your grace, your mercy, your holiness—all the aspects of your character that make you beautiful.

Worth

Unmatched Value   DAY 1

Consider the lilies, how they grow: they neither toil nor spin, yet I tell you, even Solomon in all his glory was not arrayed like one of these.

Luke 12:27

This week I read through Peter's letters to the Christian church, a nice change of pace from Paul's letters. Most encouraging to me was the relationship between the joy of our salvation and our faith.

These have come so that the proven genuineness of your faith—of greater worth than gold, which perishes even though refined by fire—may result in praise, glory and honor when Jesus Christ is revealed. Though you have not seen him, you love him; and even though you do not see him now, you believe in him and are filled with an inexpressible and glorious joy, for you are receiving the end result of your faith, the salvation of your souls.

1 Peter 1:7–9 NIV

As I write this reflection, gold is valued at $1,565 per ounce. That's about $25,000 per pound. The typical gold bar used in trading weighs four hundred ounces (about twenty-five pounds), which totals $626,000. Throughout history, gold has always maintained its special value—it is precious, an economic standard that does not waver like common currency.

When gold is used in the Bible it represents unmatched value, unprecedented permanence, ultimate superiority, and security. Peter compares gold to faith in Christ. Our faith is tested much like gold is refined by fire. Peter says our faith is actually more valuable than gold—that most precious and rarest of metals—because gold will fade with the earth, but our faith will remain.

Our faith will encounter testing, a refinement, if you will. But our faith, unlike gold, is eternally permanent. It is based on the Superior One. It secures us. It is matchless in the world because it is based on Christ's redeeming work on the cross—the joy of our salvation!

This is why we have inexpressible joy in the midst of difficulties and trials—because our salvation points us toward a time when we will enjoy Christ in the fullest. Peter says that even the angels "long to look into these things" (1 Peter 1:12 NIV). What joy! What precious faith!

Today, continue on. Stay in the race. Hold tightly to your most precious faith—that confidence of what we hope for, that surety of what we can't see. In your hardships, remember the goal of your faith: Christ, the source of our salvation.

Today's Prayer

Lord Jesus, I pray the words of Peter today: "And after you have suffered a little while, the God of all grace, who has called you to his eternal glory in Christ, will himself restore, confirm, strengthen, and establish you. To him be the dominion forever and ever. Amen."[1]

I Am Violent and Lost   DAY 2

Keep a firm grip on the faith.

1 Peter 5:9 THE MESSAGE

I found myself out upon the waters, the waves and breakers crashing. I left my fear back inside the boat, and my trust unfolded in front of me—a trust without borders.

A holy presence circled around me, calling me further into the unknown.

But Jesus did not appear out of the darkness. He didn't walk across the stormy waters.

Or did he, and I couldn't see above the waves? Was I sinking? Drowning? Was my soul in peril, consumed by my doubt?

Be wary; doubt looks like our everyday—it's the familiar and the safe, it's the known and the controlled.

Today's Prayer

Lord Jesus, doubt crowds in and lies to me. Speak your truth to me. I want to walk upon the waters, but I need the confidence found in your love.

Attend to Me   DAY 3

Today's Prayer

Lord Jesus, what can I say to you that you will come to my side today? "Attend unto my cry, give ear unto my prayer, that goeth not out of feigned lips."[2] *Bend your ear low to me, so that you can hear me today, for I feel worthless. I am next to nothing. O to be your lily in the open field today.*

Pick me up out of the pit! Show me your lovingkindness today, O my Lord.

Water Walking   DAY 4

Jumping out of the boat, Peter walked on the water to Jesus.

Matthew 14:29 THE MESSAGE

Water walking, like the kind Peter did in this passage of Matthew, sticks out in my reality. How about yours? It makes no sense, and, many times, neither does faith. Faith finds us lost and violent, yet alive. It carries us toward our love, the object of eternal goodness. Faith prompts us from our safe little boats, out onto the open waters.

It's only out on the open waters, in the violent mystery of the unknown, that my faith finds resonance—echoing into the realm of the above. Faith seems dangerous, even scary. "Voices are in the wind!" we cry. But it's not a ghost; it is Christ already walking on the heaving waves. No need to be afraid! He's calling for you and me to join him.

"But I hear muted screams—faith is too dangerous!"

But the screams you hear are just your own, because you took your eye off of him and you are drowning. The voice you hear is singular, and it is calling through your drowning, through my drowning. He finds you and me flailing, calms our arms, and sets us upon the waves.

The world ends for most in a trickling whimper. Oh, how we love to let the waves overcome. Our doubt drowns us.

But not for me, not today. Today I will run up the waves and skid down their swells. For I am a water walker.

Today's Prayer

Lord Jesus, I want to surf the waves of this world with you today. I want to walk out with you in the wildest winds and among the breakers. I can never drown when I water walk with you.

Into the Above   DAY 5

By his divine power, God has given us everything we need for living a godly life. We have received all of this by coming to know him, the one who called us to himself by means of his marvelous glory and excellence.

2 Peter 1:3 NLT

Lord, I will flail and rise, but only because your hand seized mine. You pulled me up and threw me into the mysterious above, where your fiery messengers sing in rapt worship.

I know well enough how the wind blows this way and that. I hear it rustling through the trees, but I have no idea where it comes from or where it's headed next. I take comfort in the fact that I am born from the wind, I am a spirit walker—walking in your Holy Spirit with *numinous* force and beauty. And that is where I find my preciousness, my worth.

You have given me everything, Lord! By knowing you, I gleam in the darkness. You stretched out your glory unto me and made me shimmer with a weight and fascination only given by your power and wonder.

Today's Prayer

Lord Jesus, who am I? I am yours. I am yours.

Wonder

Things Too Wonderful

> Therefore I have uttered what I did not understand, things too wonderful for me, which I did not know.
>
> Job 42:3

Job uttered the words above after God asked in his great inquisition, "Who has preceded Me, that I should repay him?" (Job 41:11 NKJV).

Our trials in this life are real. But when we cast our trials up against God, how do they compare? There is so much we do not understand, things too wonderful for our minds and hearts and eyes to see and know.

How do we find comfort in the midst of great pain and loss?

God told Job that he made the Leviathan, in all his fierce and awful glory. Why would he make such a fear-inducing creature? As a reminder: *God's goodness and magnificence encompass everything, from the lily to the Leviathan.*

It's not that we *have* to understand our trials and life-pain. Rather, it is that we believe that God will cover, that God is good, that God is wonderful—too wonderful.

Words and prayers seem insignificant when pain sits with us at the breakfast table, when we must endure day in and day out. But remember, he who created the Leviathan also created the lily, and he cares deeply for both. How much more will he care for you, dear sister, dear brother?

Today's Prayer
Lord Jesus, in your strength and wonder we rest, O King, Lord of heaven and earth. Give us the strength to endure and the wisdom to see into your wonder.

Who *Is* This God? DAY 2

Then the Lord answered Job from the whirlwind.

Job 38:1 NLT

Yesterday I spoke with a dear friend who had some very real questions about God—the damning God. You know the one. How difficult it is to hold up the God of the Old Testament and the one embodied in the Jesus of the New Testament.

But when I begin way back, all the way back to before he spoke light and darkness and you and me into existence, all the way back to the avian image of him hovering over the deep, I see nothing. For what business does my imagination have there at all? Who is this God that he would choose to create, thinking silently over a primordial glob anticipating my existence?

Who is this God speaking light and darkness, you and me? Who is this God walking like a hurricane through the garden of Eden with his most prized creation—you and me? Who is this God mingling with us? What could he possibly want from us? What does he expect? Does he experience joy with Adam? Does he laugh with Eve?

Who is this God who sets boundaries, knowing that we—humankind—will step beyond them? Is he the God uncommon? Is he a God so good his very nature can have nothing to do with the slightest shadow of pride—the unhim? Who is this God who loves us so much as to release us to our own whims, our own lusts, our own selves? What is this path away from him? Does it not lead to destruction?

Today's Prayer

Lord Jesus, help me understand you—the world-giving you and the damning you. I am bracing myself so that I can understand and fathom what you will say.

Brace Yourself   DAY 3

Today's Prayer

Lord Jesus, we know you are good, but at times we feel too small amidst the wonder of it all—we feel insignificant. Remind us how Job gathered himself in order to use all his faculties to plumb the depths of your wonder, your glory—all of you.

Lord God, you do not wave your God-banner like a bully, you encourage us to dive into you, but warn us that it may hurt and it may be confusing and we may feel insignificant at times. All is well, for you will help me, you will hold me. Hold me now, my Lord and my God.

A Wondrous Love   DAY 4

> So the Lord God banished him from the Garden of Eden to
> work the ground from which he had been taken. After he drove
> the man out, he placed on the east side of the Garden of Eden
> cherubim and a flaming sword flashing back and forth to guard
> the way to the tree of life.
>
> Genesis 3:23–24 NIV

Even in Sunday school, I remember feeling sad that God
kicked Adam and Eve out of the garden after they sinned. I
can still see the illustrations the teacher used for Adam and Eve
and the little fur coats the teacher placed on them. I even felt sad
about the coats, because they represented God killing animals.

For years, I never thought any deeper about that scene, until
one evening I was researching a book project. What I passed over
as a boy in Sunday school I now understand more deeply. Because
Adam and Eve sinned, they had to face the consequences of their
actions—expulsion from the garden. But what *is* the garden?

The garden is, in many ways, a precursor for the synagogue
and, later, the temple. Not only was it a physical place filled with
God's provision and abundance, but it was a spiritual dwelling
as well. God's presence literally filled the garden.

Just before God discovers Adam and Eve and their sinful
deception, the Scriptures depict God walking in the cool of the
evening. Some commentaries suggest that God walking through
the garden would have been like a cool hurricane wind blowing
through the garden. Adam, at once, would have known God
was coming near. God walked with Adam and Eve. He spoke
with them. The garden was, therefore, a beautiful place filled
with abundance and also God himself. So it was a place of intimacy. And God drove them away from it—away from him at
the deepest level.

So sin caused a grand separation between God and humankind. I know that seems like Bible Study 101, but it's easy to gloss over the intimacy lost. Let your imagination fill in some cracks in the story of God creating Adam and Eve and their ensuing relationship and subsequent separation. This isn't just a lesson in right doctrine; it's the beginning of a love story.

Today's Prayer
Lord Jesus, I am caught in the wonder of your deep love for me, how you desire intimacy with me. Thank you for loving me.

His Beloved Heirs   DAY 5

And the Lord God made clothing from animal skins for Adam and his wife.

Genesis 3:21 NLT

After God expelled Adam and Eve from his presence, he, in essence, made a promise to them. And this promise is more than simply clothing the naked humans, who now knew they were naked and were ashamed. I always thought God was acting out of propriety, but it turns out to be a gesture full of wonder and love.

Readers in the ancient Near East would read this text with profound curiosity. God expels Adam and Eve, then kills some beasts and makes clothing for them. In the ancient Near East, when a master or a father gives a robe to his child, it symbolizes inheritance. When Joseph was given the "amazing technicolor dreamcoat," his father was telling him: *Everything I have is yours. You are my heir.*

So even though God kicks his favorite creation from the garden, he does not disavow them. On the contrary, he says, "Though I am sending you away from my presence, I love you and have so much planned for you. All I have is yours, for you are still my beloved."

God's beast-killing was, indeed, a beautiful act of love, reminding Adam and Eve that they still represent him in the world because they remain his children.

Too often we make the Bible into a doctrine dispenser. And yes, it is to be used for doctrine and teaching and reproof. But it is a love story at its core. Just like God placed clothing on humankind to say, "You're mine, and I'm coming for you," he also placed inside each one of us a desire to be reconciled with him as well.

We feel the tinge of joy when we see a sunset or when we find satisfaction in our work, or when we experience forgiveness within a relationship. Something exists in those experiences (and so many others), it points us to a deeper place, and like St. Augustine said, our souls remain restless until they find their home in God. We yearn to get back in the garden.

Today's Prayer
Lord Jesus, thank you for coming after me.

Worship

An Unveneered Encounter   DAY 1

> My sacrifice, O God, is a broken spirit; a broken and contrite heart you, God, will not despise.
>
> Psalm 51:17 NIV

In 2000 I shunned the new "worship movement." Part of an acoustic band myself, I grew cynical of the pomp and show accompanying new worship music. I wanted things stripped down, naked and without guile. But did I not simply desire a different, contrasting method myself?

What is important when it comes to music and worship?

I believe the method must fit the message, but more than method, I believe it is an unveneered encounter with God. How far will we go to fabricate an *experience* that feeds our sensual desires when what God desires is an authentic encounter?

Let us today consider our own desires when it comes to worship music. The central focus of worship is God himself, not a personal preference in music. Is my spirit broken and contrite before God? Have I clouded my intimacy with the Almighty with a personal preference that really has no bearing on whether or not God receives the praise he deserves?[1]

Today's Prayer

*Lord Jesus, what I offer you today is my life in worship.
No music, no preference, only a broken and humble spirit.
My eyes turn to you, my King and my God. To you alone
do I lift up the song of my heart in praise.*

A Sinai Experience   DAY 2

Not that we are sufficient in ourselves to claim anything as coming from us, but our sufficiency is from God, who has made us sufficient to be ministers of a new covenant, not of the letter but of the Spirit. For the letter kills, but the Spirit gives life.

2 Corinthians 3:5–6

I believe there are those leaders among us—worship leaders, pastors, artists, poets, dancers—who have been to Sinai. They have returned with the glow of Moses, and they communicate that brilliance with song (and art, poetry, and dance). We watch them climb into the cleft of the rock and reach out for God as he passes by. We *feel* them reaching, and think we can fabricate that same feeling, that same reaching, without ourselves going up to the mountain.

This really comes to light on Sunday mornings when worship leaders attempt to fabricate the same emotions they see in other leaders—leaders who have actually encountered God and been changed.

What is the result of such fabrication? A mimed worship experience on Sundays, devoid of true encounter. Moses *talked* with the Lord. He *inquired* of the Lord. He *pushed* on the Lord. And the Lord himself passed by—Moses *saw* him, if only his back.

We cannot take others to a place we have not been to ourselves. Leaders in the church must be vigilant in the cultivation of their intimacy with God. A fabricated worship experience is no worship experience at all. Rather, it is pure emotionalism.

Though I am using the worship leader as an example here because it is so prevalent, we all can learn from the principle at hand: We cannot take others to a place we've never been. Plug that principle into your Bible study group at school, your women's Bible study at church, your small group, your children at home.

Pull your eyes away from websites and television broadcasts of conferences, stop attending grand conferences loaded with professional Christians, and get out and under the mystery of God himself. If you pursue him the way that he pursues you, you will find yourself with eyes closed approaching Sinai. And when you open your eyes and look behind you, you'll see those who have dared to follow you.

Today's Prayer

Lord Jesus, how wonderful to possess the boldness of Moses, who said, "Let me see you, Lord. Let me see your glory!"

A Life Given   DAY 3

Today's Prayer

Lord Jesus, "Let us overcome by our manner of living rather than by our words alone. For this is the main battle, this is the unanswerable argument, the argument from conduct. For though we give ten thousand precepts of philosophy in words, if we do not exhibit a life better than theirs, the gain is nothing. For it is not what is said that draws their attention, but what we do, and they say, 'Do you first obey your own words, and then admonish others. . . .' Let us win them therefore by our life."[2]

Thirst for Brilliance   DAY 4

And we all, who with unveiled faces contemplate the Lord's glory, are being transformed into his image with ever-increasing glory, which comes from the Lord, who is the Spirit.

2 Corinthians 3:18 NIV

What would our Sunday gatherings turn into if, on these Little Easters, we climbed into the cleft of the rock and huddled as God's children, craning our necks just to catch a glimpse of our Father? What if our thirst was not for the sensual experience but for the brilliance of God's glory, covering our lives like the summer gleam?

It's not enough to mime the holy encounters of others. We must approach the mountain, cast away our fear and insecurity, and fall on our faces. Then and only then will we find our way up the mountain.

Guard your steps when you go to the house of God. To draw near to listen is better than to offer the sacrifice of fools, for they do not know that they are doing evil. Be not rash with your mouth, nor let your heart be hasty to utter a word before God, for God is in heaven and you are on earth. Therefore let your words be few.

Ecclesiastes 5:1–2

After your chaotic struggle to make it to church this Sunday, breathe. Walk into your own tent of meeting and *listen*. In the quiet the Lord speaks. As you stand within his quiet, gather boldness, gather your fears, gather your broken pieces, and ask him . . . go ahead, ask him: Lord, will you show me your glory?

Then hear his heart: "Hide here, dear child. I will pass by, and you will see me. After I pass, show your brothers and sisters— not in a show, but with the sweetness of your life and evidence of Spirit rummaging through your soul."

Today's Prayer

Lord Jesus, I want to see your glory. I want to encounter you.

Lines to Loved Ones   DAY 5

Now the Lord is the Spirit, and where the Spirit of the Lord is, there is freedom.

2 Corinthians 3:17

*T*o my brothers and sisters leading in the worship with song:
Through the gray and white clouds I thought of you, my friends whom I love. And this morning, my prayer is for you and for worship. I don't know who is leading and who is listening in the shadows behind, but I pray the Lord bless you and keep you, that his face would shine upon you in all its celestial holiness and light, radiant as the sun and beautiful as the morning star.

People are dying to trek up Mount Sinai—they thirst for an authentic worship experience through the beauty of music. But they cannot journey with a leader who has not been there. So this morning, in the dark and in the coffee aroma and in the kids screaming on the way to church and in the tension of the politics of a church that is still his bride, go to Sinai and reach out for him . . . reach for him from the shadow of the cleft and pray you don't die.

And at the same time you pray for life, reach out and seize holiness—a holiness able to clothe you and keep you, renew you from trouble, and give you life ever-new, evermore.[3]

Today's Prayer

Lord Jesus, protect our worship leaders. Give them your sight. Show them your glory and strengthen them to lead us to it.

Longing

We Drink the Now and Forever

The Lord is good to those who wait for him, to the soul who seeks him.

Lamentations 3 25

Anticipation works its magic on us as longing propels us toward our lovers. It creates that simmering in the pit of your stomach that feels like hunger but is never satisfied. We think about the next time we'll see our beloved or our children when we're away. The magnetism of their lives somehow compounds our own existence. Finally the union of physical bodies codifies the spiritual connection. At once our hunger is kept in abeyance.

The love of another, like a river, fills and does not stop filling, as it is fed from the high mountain springs that tap in to the infinity of our Father.

Without *longing* we cease to move forward. Indeed, a life without longing reflects the dark edges of despair—that place where death is hoped for while knowing that death cannot come. Even in our despair we long.

Then can it be that nothing escapes longing? Can it be that our propeller toward infinity is the heart of Infinity himself. Is longing God himself?

Or perhaps it is the action of longing and the subject of longing all at once. Perhaps when we arrive at the gates of heaven and succumb to God's overwhelming presence we will cease to long for that something we really can't explain. Perhaps we will, like the characters in C. S. Lewis's *The Last Battle,* gallop into eternity exclaiming, "Further up and further in!"

And that's it, isn't it? When we finally enter into heaven, we will finally enter fully into God. We will be fully known, and we will know, fully. We will gallop into him and he will never end. "More of you, Jesus!" we will exclaim, and he will shout back to us, "Come further, little ones! You have only just begun!"

We will in that moment dig in our spurs and ride our stallions into the high mountains, down through the cascading valleys of forevermore; the trees and rocks and waterfalls ringing with, "Holy, holy, holy!" And the light that drowns the horizon will never fully set but gleam in a state of perpetual setting. There will be nothing for us to think at that moment, for we will spin into tomorrow as we ride, and spin again into the tomorrow even as we drink the *now and forever.*

Our tears will smear in the wind and mingle with the river, and, like children again, we will run naked into grassy fields and sing the song of the dandelions' flight.

It is the cynic who derides the one who is "so heavenly minded they are of no earthly good." For we must *long for something* to be of any good use in this world.

Blessed are they who hunger and thirst for righteousness. Blessed are they who seek with all their hearts. Blessed are they who never stop running toward the longing in their hearts. For they shall inherit eternal longing and never thirst.

Today's Prayer
Lord Jesus, I pray for you to come. Yes, come, Lord Jesus, come.

Taste for the Other DAY 2

"I am the Alpha and the Omega," says the Lord God, "who is and who was and who is to come, the Almighty."

Revelation 1:8

What is it about this world that we love? We love it so much we often mistake it for the *true* thing we ought to love. And it is really no thing at all. It is, indeed, Christ himself—the ever-present *Logos*, who breathed the foundations of the world into existence. Might it be that breath we feel that makes us love this earth and everything in it?

The spring rain giving way to the cherry blossoms; the deep summer nights alive with the sound and the fury of life; the color and smell of autumn with its frost-laden mornings and beckoning horizon; the solace of winter and the congregating of friends around a fire. Maybe your loves for this world are different. Name them now, as you read. You love it here. And that is as it should be.

But what happens when we forget that the soul of the seasons is the breath of Christ? What happens when we forget we were not only placed into this world but also made for another? We touched on this in an earlier reading, but in his philosophical allegory *The Pilgrim's Regress*, C. S. Lewis uses the phrase "taste for the other." Our "taste for the other" defines our humanity. When we lose it, we lose our humanity.

Today's Prayer

Lord Jesus, it's when I am at my worst that I realize how far I've drifted from you—even desiring you. Restore my humanity. Restore my wholeness. Restore my taste for you and all that you are. You are good, and true, and righteous. You are holy, and beautiful, and pure. I am hungry for you, Lord.

The Ravishing Cool   DAY 3

Today's Prayer

Lord Jesus, I want to trust you so I can live confidently in my desire, knowing it is yours. How glorious to live in the desires of my heavenly Father, who wants nothing more than to bless his children, to give every good and perfect gift to those who seek him with all their heart, mind, soul, and strength.

Here I am, O my Lord, in the gray autumn morning, stirring my cup while trying to stir my heart for you. So much of today weighs down on my shoulders. If I think too long, I am overwhelmed.

But the clouds of today do not hold sway over me, for your beauty and tenderness climb after me. And if I'm aware enough, the simple, small joys in life point to you. The innocence of a child's smile, the ravishing cool, they both point to you.

For you hold all things together. You hold me together. And today, I need you to hold me together. I need you to hold me.

Reiterated Pleasures   DAY 4

I want to know you, Lord, and the power of your resurrection.

Philippians 3:10

(my paraphrase)

As he stood pondering over this and wondering how often in his life on earth he had reiterated pleasures not through desire, but in the teeth of desire and in obedience to a spurious rationalism.

C. S. Lewis, *Perelandra*[1]

What is the difference between experiencing pleasure "through desire" and experiencing pleasure "in the teeth of desire"? Perhaps the difference is the same as having a glass or two of wine versus alcoholism. Or transfer anything that can be good but bent into bad. Only, let us look past this and into desire itself.

How can we live reiterating pleasures through desire?

In his essay "The Weight of Glory," C. S. Lewis challenges our desires, calling them too weak. And that concerns me. Are my desires for the Lord this morning too weak? Do I slap around in the mud because my desires come from it?

The more I know God, and this power, the more the pleasures in this life stem from *his desires*. And there I am, clothed in him and not in the teeth of my own muddy lusts.

Today's Prayer

Lord Jesus, help me to stand up and step from my mudhole into the glory of your desire.

From the Mudhole   DAY 5

Declare his glory . . .

Psalm 96:3

How do I rise from my mudhole? When my desires fail to shimmer in the light of his glory, I must *see*. And by see I mean I must live aware: aware of myself—my spirit and whatever cloaks it with the heaviness of sin.

Too often I find the answer in one simple word: *thankfulness*. Do my desires falter because I long for nothing? No. They falter because I am seeking the wrong things. Greed seeds itself in my gut and grows into a pesky stomach virus. I want, I want, I want, but it's all the mud, not the glory.

When I live with open hands and not with a clenched fist, I live content. I am thankful because I realize the desire does not rise or fall based upon my greed. Rather, it alights to my spirit when I, daily, give to the Lord his due.

Splendor and majesty are before him; strength and glory are in his sanctuary. . . . Ascribe to the Lord glory and strength. Ascribe to the Lord the glory due his name. . . . Worship the Lord in the splendor of his holiness; tremble before him, all the earth.

Psalm 96:6–9 NIV

And there it is: ascribe, worship, tremble. These are our marching orders today. They help our desires because they have nothing to do with the haughty desires of the flesh. They help because they soar.

If you want to soar, give flight to thankfulness. Live aware of what weighs you down, and worship God where you sit or stand. Feel the mud drip off as you rise in soaring praise.

Today's Prayer

Lord Jesus, I give you every breath in my lungs today. I worship and adore you. I kneel and tremble before you. I rest in thanks, for you who are so holy and mighty lift me up on the wings of eagles. And I soar.

Forgiveness

Forgiveness Is Hard

> And forgive us our sins; for we ourselves forgive everyone who is indebted to us.
>
> Luke 11:4

Do you have trouble forgiving people?

I had to ask my five-year-old daughter for forgiveness a few days ago. I knelt beside her as she was working on a puzzle. "Lyric, will you forgive me?" She looked up from her puzzle pieces and, without hesitating, said, "I forgive you, Daddy. Wanna help me with my puzzle?"

Just like that. I was forgiven. All was forgotten and we finished the puzzle together. That same day I stumbled upon a short essay by C. S. Lewis titled, "On Forgiveness." In the essay, Lewis says that many of us don't really *believe* in the forgiveness of sins like we say we do. Rather than ask God for forgiveness, we often only ask him to excuse us.

Our lack of belief in forgiveness carries over into our relationships with others. What about that person who betrayed you? Have you truly forgiven them, or merely excused them? To forgive, remember, is to wipe it away forever.

"But," you say, "you don't know what he did to me—how deeply I was cut by his actions!"

That is precisely what forgiveness is for: It sees the depth of God's forgiveness for us and empowers us to bestow the same depth of forgiveness upon others. No excuses. "To be a Christian," writes Lewis, "means to forgive the inexcusable, because God has forgiven the inexcusable in you."[1]

Our trespasses will only be forgiven to the extent that we forgive others. How can we say we believe in forgiveness of our own sins and yet not offer the same forgiveness to others?

Seventy times seven we are to forgive—the daily transgressions against us and from us. Who do you need to forgive today?

Do you really believe in forgiveness of sins? If so, your belief will be evidenced in how deeply you forgive those who have wronged you. That's the deal.

Today's Prayer

Lord Jesus, I believe in forgiveness because I stand in the assurance of your forgiveness. Help me forgive as I have been forgiven.

What Is Forgiveness? DAY 2

And whenever you stand praying, forgive, if you have anything against anyone, so that your Father also who is in heaven may forgive you your trespasses.

Mark 11:25

One night I stood around a fire pit with my brother-in-law and a couple of lifelong friends. The wind swirled smoke in our eyes and the cold bit our toes while we dug into a discussion on forgiveness.

What is it exactly? Is it a process? Is it a singular act followed by the hard road of restitution—reestablishing that which is broken in the relationship?

I think the best we did at answering our questions came from C. S. Lewis: "Forgiveness is hard."

Yes, it is. Thanks, Jack.

Relationships don't shut off when we power down our phones and laptops. They don't reboot on their own when the new year begins. They demand constant maintenance. We must turn the wrenches of love and grace, mercy and forgiveness to keep our relationships running well.

Today's Prayer

Lord Jesus, I struggle to forgive people, especially those closest to me. Help me take a first step today and begin the maintenance due to the relationships that matter most in my life. Show me whom I need to forgive.

Gracious Love   DAY 3

Today's Prayer

Lord Jesus, you are merciful and gracious, slow to anger and abounding in steadfast love.

You will not always chide, nor will you keep your anger forever.

You do not deal with me according to my sins, nor repay me according to my iniquities.

For as high as the heavens are above the earth, so great is your steadfast love toward those who fear you;

as far as the east is from the west, so far do you remove my transgressions from me.

adapted from Psalm 103:8–12

Release   DAY 4

Judge not, and you will not be judged; condemn not, and you will not be condemned; forgive, and you will be forgiven.

Luke 6:37

One definition for forgiveness in the New Testament is "release." When we forgive one another, we release one another of the transgression that divides. It's gone, like letting go of a helium balloon. Sure, you could carry that balloon around with you, looking at it and talking about it. But when you release it, the balloon disappears—carried away to God knows where.

As Christians we are forgiveness bearers in a world that yearns to be reconciled. And being a forgiveness bearer begins by seeking out friends and relatives who need release. How do you show the world how much God longs to be reconciled with it? You reconcile yourself to those closest to you.

Today's Prayer

Lord Jesus, reveal to me those whom I need to forgive. Show me the wrongs I have left unreconciled.

Dissolved   DAY 5

Blessed is the one whose transgression is forgiven, whose sin
is covered.

Psalm 32:1

Which of your relationships hangs in an unforgiving limbo?
Get out your relational wrenches, pick up the phone, or
get in your car, and get dirty in the loving relational maintenance
of forgiveness. Remember your own forgiveness and the mystery
of that reality. Though you and I deserved nothing, God pursued
us and showered forgiveness upon our rebellious hearts.

May our trust be like the psalmist's: "For you, O Lord, are
good and forgiving, abounding in steadfast love to all who call
upon you. You forgave the iniquity of your people; you covered
all their sin. Suddenly the pressure was gone—my guilt dissolved,
my sin disappeared."[2]

Today's Prayer

*Lord Jesus, I acknowledge my sin to you, and I do not cover
my iniquity. I said, "I will confess my transgressions to the
Lord," and you forgave the iniquity of my sin.*

Imagination

Our Cosmic Story

God's Spirit brooded like a bird above the watery abyss.

Genesis 1:1 THE MESSAGE

When I was a young boy I heard stories about the end of time. Always the end of time, rarely the beginning, but I loved hearing them just the same. Grand images of dragons and fiery angels and bloody horsemen of the Apocalypse littered my mind. I collected the end of time in a mythical narrative and stowed it away in my boyhood memory.

I waited for the dragon. I still wait.

Growing up in the shadow of dragons' wings left me pining for the bright light just beyond the shadow's edge. It was the light of the beginning. It stirred my imagination and made me squint, like waking from a midsummer's nap and walking into the backyard—stumbling in the wash of sunshine.

If the end of time vaulted so mythical and wonderful, I thought, then what transpired at the beginning of time must transcend my wildest dreams.

I was not disappointed.

The images from my boyhood now mingle with my adult eyes and mind. I'm all grown up now and love to read and reread the beautiful creation narrative in Genesis.

"In the beginning, God created the heavens and the earth."

Verse one begins a crescendo, the dynamic arc inviting me to eavesdrop on the Artist, who has evidently been painting for some time—the canvas before him gleaming with fresh oils.

God hovered over the waters of the deep. The avian image pitches God like an eagle spreading his wings over the void earth. The earth's story begins doused in poetry—the concise form of story. We find images of God speaking the world into existence.

The winged Spirit watches over the uninhabited primordial glob. Then, in the first cosmic sound, God's voice rings out, exhaling words in a heavenly tongue, "Let there be light."

He called everything good. Then he fashioned humans—all lumpy and dirty—and they were "very good." Then he rested.

Consider the crescendo of the beginning of time. You are that crescendo. You are that first thought of God. You are breathed into existence as the planets are sent spinning. In the beginning was the Word, and the Word was with God, and the Word was God. And in that Word, came you.

Today's Prayer

Lord Jesus, I am humbled to think how you spoke me into life as the crescendo of your masterpiece. I am blessed to find purpose brimming from the depths of your imagination.

Story Obsession   DAY 2

I came that they may have life and have it abundantly.

John 10:10

The Sunday school stories from my childhood are well behind me, but I still interact with the creation story like a child—excited to turn the page. As an adult I now understand that God's Word, though it contains stories of different literary genres and acts as a collective story, is more concerned about my position before YHWH. The divine *Logos* (God's living Word) not only helps me understand God more deeply, it helps me understand my desperate need for his redemption.

Our culture obsesses over story. Some encourage us to live our best lives now, or to make our life story epic. Some even try to tell a "better story" than what the Scriptures offer. My friend Jason says the Christian ethos around storytelling is like when we were kids and thought if we covered our eyes, no one would see us because we could not see them—we think the story is all about us.

But the cosmic story does not revolve around us. The biblical narrative, though it does frame us as God's bride and lover and players in the cosmic play, revolves around YHWH and his pursuit of you and me. It is for his glory—not ours—that we live and breathe and have our being. He is the main character. I am not.

Today I am reminded that God is our hero: He creates with mere words and loves us enough to enter the narrative he sketched so that we are not turned to ash by the dragon.

Today's Prayer

Lord Jesus, I want to revisit the beginning—how you thought this universe into existence, including me. You are the author and finisher of my faith.

God in the Lines   DAY 3

Today's Prayer

Lord Jesus, make me to know your ways. Teach me your paths. Lead me in your truth and teach me, for you are the God of my salvation; for you I wait all the day long.

Symbols of Wonder   DAY 4

But sanctify the Lord God in your hearts, and always be ready to give a defense to everyone who asks you a reason for the hope that is in you, with meekness and fear.

1 Peter 3:15 NKJV

Even though we must remain vigilant to keep the narrative of Scripture focused on God and not twist the gospel to be an empowerment tool for ourselves, we cannot deny we live in a culture driven by story, and for good reason. Stories ignite our imaginations. Stories give meaning to truths we might otherwise not understand. Some of our most loved stories are allegories or myths that communicate a transcendent "something."

C. S. Lewis said the imagination works in tandem with rationality as the vehicle of meaning. "In other words, although one cannot discuss anything intelligently without the use of reason, the metaphorical condition of language, particularly theological language, necessitates that the highest truths be expressed in symbols which are not rationally but imaginatively understood."[1] Too often we err on the side of rationality and American pragmatism when it comes to truth. In the past, apologists debated skeptics on purely rational grounds. But where do imaginative apologetics come into play? If people divine understanding by way of symbols and metaphors, then why do we persist in rational arguments?

Is this too much for a daily reflection? Well, I suppose I can only discuss with you what I myself find to be challenging and encouraging, and this is something we all can not only agree upon (I believe) but contribute to as well.

Think of the chain reaction when you encounter the beautiful in your daily life. Perhaps you wake to a soaring sunrise. It sparks your wonder. It tingles you with numinous feelings. As a Christian, you focus those feelings on your personal worship of Jesus Christ; you see his attributes within the natural wonder, and you praise him. Might beauty as an apologetic have a similar effect on someone who is looking for answers or looking for meaning?

Today's Prayer

Lord Jesus, help me to see beauty. Help me to grasp your meaning in this life so that I can communicate it imaginatively to my friends and to the world.

The Light of Imagination   DAY 5

I am the light of the world. Whoever follows me will not walk in darkness, but will have the light of life.

John 8:12

Light scatters throughout the Scriptures. Moses finds himself caught up in the light of God's presence, and Paul calls the believer a child of the kingdom of light. The mystery writer of Hebrews calls Jesus the exact radiance of God—a second sun from heaven itself.

In this famous passage in John's Gospel (8:12), we find one of the "I AM" sayings in the book. But what does Jesus *mean* when he refers to himself as the light of the world? Imagine the scene. It is the Feast of Tabernacles. Torches light up the entire city. In the temple, in the court of women, a candle lighting ceremony was held symbolizing the pillar of fire that guided the Israelites. There was singing and dancing. In this context Jesus says, "I am the light of the world." Like the torches lining the streets to help people stay on the path, Jesus offers himself to all the nations. He is the guiding light.

In order to communicate truth to his hearers, Jesus employed imagery and symbols, which already carried great meaning. We may not always realize it, but our imaginations fire our intellects. We therefore must take care to steward our imaginations well. What shapes and cultivates our imaginations: music, films, books, or one of many other things? How do we use our imaginations in our witness for Christ?

Jesus is the light of the world. Through him, we can truly see everything else. When C. S. Lewis converted to Christianity, he says that the conversion actually began years earlier when he read the book *Phantastes* by the Scottish writer and theologian George MacDonald. Lewis says that as he read it, it was as if his imagination were being baptized. He began to see everything in the world in a new and holy light.

Today, think about your imagination. Has it been truly baptized? Has the light of Christ shone through it, giving you a new outlook? Or have you allowed the fanciful things of the world to lure you from the path lit by the light of Christ?

Today's Prayer

Lord Jesus, I see you now, my Light of lights. Baptize my imagination all over again. Keep my light shining with imaginative gleam and alluring wonder.

Pain

Scream Your Pain

> Serve the Lord with fear, and rejoice with trembling.
>
> Psalm 2:11

Have you ever called up your closest friend and said, "Hey, I need someone to talk to. Can I come over?" When you meet, you admit to your friend that you just need to vent—you need someone who'll listen to you work out some pain.

For the next hour you unravel emotions and naked truths from the depths of your heart. Your friend, meanwhile, sits and nods.

Maybe there are tears. Maybe there's vitriol. Maybe you utter words and ideas that, if anyone else heard, would cause them to question your faith and sanity. After you finish, you flop down in a chair in a heap of confusion and pain, but also relief. Your friend, then, wraps his or her arms around you and says nothing—just holds you.

If our friends can provide an emotional haven, how much more, then, can God provide for us?

Unfortunately, I think some people view God less as a patient and understanding friend and more like a massive unfeeling omnipotent God—a divine being who offers little more than a "Just deal with it," when pain pushes us down.

At the end of the book of Job, God tells this broken man to "brace yourself like a man; I will question you, and you shall hear me." It's easy, and quite common, to view this exchange between God and Job as a cosmic beat down: "Yeah, you're suffering, but did you create all this? Well, then . . ."

But this interpretation of the nature of their discussion and God's tone couldn't be further from this negative perspective. It's easy to read Scripture and respond to what is written. But here we must also notice what is not there.

Throughout the book, Job pleads for vindication. He curses the day he was born and he complains and unleashes an emotional onslaught to God. But God does not say, "Okay, little broken man—shut it and stand in awe of me." He doesn't browbeat Job at all.

Rather, he *allows* Job to vent. Then he says, "Now, Job . . . gather your strength as a man and see if you can—with that strength—understand the height and depth of my being—how I hold everything from the beautiful to the silly to the ridiculous to the ugly to the marvelous to the insignificant in the palm of my hand. And you, Job, are chief among it all."

Today's Prayer

Lord Jesus, today I need to vent my emotions. Grant me the grace and mercy to be honest with you and the discernment to hear and heed your instruction.

Your Cursings   DAY 2

I know that you can do all things,
and that no purpose of yours can be thwarted.

Job 42:2

The book of Job wraps up with Job saying, "I had *heard of* you, but now *I see you*. And, in my distress am comforted in the ashes of my life." In most of our translations, 42:6 reads: "Therefore I despise myself, and repent in dust and ashes." A better word here for *repent* is "comfort." In the end, Job sees God's true character and finds comfort amid the ashes of his life.

Too often in our struggles we shy away from God. As we struggle through trials, people tell us that everything will work out for the glory of God—that we just need to be faithful and realize that God has a plan. But those words ring hollow for those in the muck of life.

Is God in control? Certainly he is. But that does not mean we don't writhe in daily pain and struggle and confusion when a trial comes our way. To those mucking through it today and the coming weeks, know this: God is big enough for your cursings and confusion, your sadness and despair, your unbelief and hopelessness, your emptiness and pain. Scream it out to him. He can take it. Don't trudge through your trial feeling like it's wrong to complain to God. That is a lie.

Sometimes the best thing we can do during affliction is vent the way we do to our friends. Afterward, a God-sized embrace waits. Through our wails and swinging fists, his embrace envelops; in our ashes, he comforts.

Today's Prayer
Lord Jesus, hold me.

The Sound in the Wake   DAY 3

Today's Prayer
Lord Jesus, calm my sea.

Today's prayer is a simple one, a timeless one especially needed when this reflection was written, the day after the horrific school shooting in Newtown, Connecticut, December 21, 2012.

Propitious answers seldom come to questions concerning tragedy. Rather, poignant reminders of our human limitations, along with the vast sea of unanswerable questions, linger. In the wake of the Sandy Hook calamity, our nation reels with heavy emotion. The naked aggression against the innocent children who lost their lives incites our most base reactions: anger, sadness, confusion.

Even as the nation cries out for answers, the families who lost *everything* must face each day, must face the media, must face the sound of silence within what should be joyful halls of their Christmas homes, must face the "Why?" that will rise from the heaving dark ocean of loss in their hearts.

God, have you not made a mistake? Have you forgotten your own?

The media dove in headfirst to tackle the so-called issues at hand: gun control, mental illness, school security. Debates will rise and inflamed political discourse will do its utmost to take this delicate and mysteriously human affair and turn it into ideological talking points. How long did it take for the gun control debate to start in your Facebook and Twitter feeds? We can't help ourselves.

We are frail—capable of brutishness and wonder. All of us pitch and recoil in the face of such stark shadows attempting to claim the day. In our hurt we feel like we should say something.

We seem to forget that grief moves like the sloth, content to cling. It does not subside when something else newsworthy occurs. You can't turn the channel from personal loss.

The shoreline of grief will always receive the ebbing tide of pain—bringing "the eternal note of sadness in."[1]

When young lives are prematurely cut down, humanity suffers and we should listen and learn. Will we only hear what Sophocles heard in the Aegean Sea, that "turbid ebb and flow of human misery"?[2] Or will we notice the lapping sound of faith?

How will faith respond to such a melancholy roar? How should it guide our engagement on the issues?

After we've hurled our rocks of doubt into the ominous sea of pain, will we then set out to walk upon those same turbulent waters?

The answers to pain rest in our hearing. For loud crashes the weight of loss upon our shifting sands, but the tide yet subsides and warm breezes blow, casting quiet like a net, enveloping.

Faith whispers upon this darkling plain, imploring us to see past waves and whitecaps and wind—out where the sun splits night in two. There a new tide churns, one bringing joy from memory. Can you hear it?

Let us listen to the whispers of faith spoken by the Christ of our redemption. And let us not forget the families. Let prayer reach out and calm the sea.

Shouting to Us   DAY 4

I cried aloud to the Lord, and he answered me from his holy hill.

Psalm 3:4

The morning tumbled on like normal, until Chris (my wife) asked me to inspect Zion's (our youngest daughter—at the time, an infant) second toe on her right foot. I found several hairs were wrapped around it. They were wrapped so tight that the upper half of her toe was purple. When I looked under her toe

I found the hairs had cut through her skin and were embedded deep into her skin. (We learned later that this "hair tourniquet" can occur when hair collects in small children's socks or their pajama footies and works its way around their toes.)

I panicked.

"Call the doctor!"

Moments later, Chris told me our pediatrician wanted to see her immediately. Now we were both panicked. Time, our doctor said, was of the essence. The next two hours were intense. Our pediatrician inspected the toe and immediately sent us across the street to Urgent Care.

A little crew was waiting for us, and for the next half hour, Zion squeezed my finger with her miniature hand and screamed as the doctors dug into her toe for the strands of hair—no anesthetic. I thought she was going to pass out. She cried and wiggled in her car seat as one doctor held her leg still, another held a giant magnifying glass, while still another fed her sugar water.

They were not able to remove all the hair, but they did get her circulation back. She wasn't going to lose half her toe. But she was still writhing in pain and bleeding, so they sent us to the ER.

Going to the ER is like stepping into a time warp. There's nothing urgent about that place.

After a numbing ointment failed to work, the doctors decided to REALLY numb it—with a needle. They reminded us that she would scream and that there are thousands of nerve endings all around our toes and that the medicine would also sting.

I was holding Zion's finger while Chris paced. Then they stuck her. I have never heard an infant scream like that. It was the wail of a seventeen-month-old mixed with something *else*—*something undefinable*. There was nothing I could do for her but hold her hand, rub her head, and wipe the tears as they streamed out of her glassy blue eyes. She had to endure it by herself. I prayed that Daddy's voice and touch would offer some kind of comfort.

They removed all the hair along with some toe tissue. After they finished, Zion passed out on the table; she slept for about twenty minutes . . . calm and exhausted. She's great today. She's sporting a nice, deep cut all around her toe, but she's smiling like it's her job.

Today's Prayer

Lord Jesus, you are always present in times of my greatest need; help me to remember you are also there in my greatest victory.

No Megaphone   DAY 5

God, your God, is striding ahead of you. He's right there with you. He won't let you down; he won't leave you.

Deuteronomy 31:6 The Message

I think sometimes suffering in this life is like screaming through a needle stick. Pain is a megaphone, and certainly God uses it— shouting to us in our pain.[3] But when I knelt beside Zion, I didn't shout anything. I whispered, "Daddy's here. I have you. It will pass . . . it will pass. I love you." Over and over I whispered this.

This is the prayer for each of us today—to those especially dealing with the needle stick of personal pain.

Today's Prayer

Lord Jesus, hold my hand today. Whisper to me. Help me through it and make it end. Catch me as I lose my strength; kiss me awake to a new morning. Stay always near me, God my Father.

Unity

Together as One

> I do not ask for these only, but also for those who will believe
> in me through their word, that they may all be one, just as you,
> Father, are in me, and I in you, that they also may be in us, so
> that the world may believe that you have sent me.
>
> John 17:20–22

To be a Christian is to be *one* with Christ, just as Christ himself is one with the Father. Our solidarity with Christ should, therefore, define us in a fragmented world. Christian unity was the theme of Christ's final prayer. It is no small thing that Christ's final thoughts center on the apologetic of unity.

But Christians love denominations. Christians love quibbling over methodologies. Christians love bickering within the ranks. Increasingly popular Christian celebrities and leaders, whether in the blogosphere or mega-pastors themselves, seek distinction from one another rather than from the world—as Jesus prayed.

"The time is always ripe for re-union," wrote C. S. Lewis. "Divisions between Christians are a sin and a scandal, and Christians ought at all times to be making contributions towards re-union, if it is only by their prayers."[1]

Today's Prayer

Lord Jesus, forgive us, the universal church, for doing more to divide than giving up to unite. Bring us together, as one, for your glory.

Abandon Your Self   DAY 2

I in them and you in me, that they may become perfectly one, so that the world may know that you sent me and loved them even as you loved me.

John 17:23

I find that I fail to pray for my fellow brothers and sisters like I should. I also do not pray as I should for Christian solidarity. One thing I do find, however, is the trail toward unity resting in abandonment of self. As I follow hard after Christ, I find the more I wrap myself in him—and thus abandon my self—the things that might otherwise cause division within my heart fall away. I am engulfed in Christ and feel the solidarity of the three-in-one grow in me a guided love—one that values truth and goodness; one that wraps me in his glory, beautifying this ugly skeleton of a man. (Thank you, Jesus!)

Each week leads to a time when believers everywhere gather to worship, as one, God the Father. As I prepare for the weekend worship gathering; as I prepare for work next week; as I prepare to engage in the fragmented world before me, I prepare for the difficult task of living in solidarity with Christ—with a living and brilliant solidarity with my brothers and sisters in Christ.

May the sentiment of Lewis's words here be our prayer as we seek daily to stand united, together as one.

Today's Prayer

Lord Jesus, "I sometimes have a bright dream of re-union engulfing us unawares, like a great wave from behind our backs, perhaps at the very moment when our official representatives are still pronouncing it impossible."[2]

A Prayer of Hope   DAY 3

Today's Prayer

Lord Jesus, your children argue and bicker, fragment and drift. How can we come back, not only to you but to one another? Teach us what it means to be a family again. Convict our hearts. Instruct our hearts on what it means to engage publicly with one another.

Grant us grace to deal with our baggage—our bad experience with church growing up, a dictatorial pastor, or an abusive "religion" gallivanting about as if it were true Christianity. You are the only One who can draw us toward one another. Do it, Lord Jesus.

Refreshment   DAY 4

He will cover you with his pinions,
and under his wings you will find refuge;
his faithfulness is a shield and buckler.

You will not fear the terror of the night,
nor the arrow that flies by day,
nor the pestilence that stalks in darkness,
nor the destruction that wastes at noonday.

Psalm 91:4–6

I needed refreshment.

So I drove to Brian's house. He's a good friend and he's also my worship pastor. We sat on the back deck with his wife while the fireflies and candles lit the dusk. A cranky possum joined us from his noisy treetop perch.

We three drank the dragon's milk of friendship, played guitar, sang "Amazing Grace," started writing a new song and talked about hallelujah. Then we sang it—"Hallelujah," over and over.

I found my way home; it was late. I took the pixies to the potty. Half asleep, they draped over my shoulder and I whispered, "I love you." Then I found sleep. The next morning I found an email string from a group of friends—each post in the string a translucent prayer held together by the gossamer strands of Holy Communion. I cried for the despair and death we all face each day. I hollered at the cynicism, the bastard god who daily rages against belief—I hate her.

"Further up and further in," my friends! We sing and hold hands, pray and cry with those we love. For what are we if not givers of love—killing ourselves daily in love to those we hold most dear.

"The sun doth not only enrich the earth with all good things," writes the old Puritan theologian Thomas Goodwin, "but glads and refreshes all with shedding immediately *its own wings* of light and warmth, which is so pleasant to behold and enjoy. And thus doth God, and Christ the Son of righteousness."[3]

It is God who spreads his wings, the avian Spirit wrapping you and me in pinions of celestial peace and holy warmth. Beneath his cowl of light our days unfold. Some days we linger in shadows; others, we sing and dance in the light of his high noon.

The days I need refreshment, I listen to friends—friends who ask how they can pray for me, friends who play guitar with me, friends who write with me, friends who start bonfires for me. I find in them God's light of renewal, his comfort transmitted through all the good things. "He will cover you with his feathers, and under his wings you will find refuge. . . ."[4]

Today's Prayer

Lord Jesus, cover me with your feathers. Let me find refuge beneath your wings. For I am in need of refreshment. I am in need of friends. I am in need of you.

The Demands of Brotherhood   DAY 5

Behold, how good and pleasant it is when brothers dwell in unity!

Psalm 133:1

It is easy to point fingers when discussing the shortage of unity. Everyone else is to blame. If only they could get along! But what about me? What about you?

I find I am most averse to Christian unity when I am focused primarily on myself. And when I'm focused on myself, God has trouble finding a seat.

Christian brotherhood (and sisterhood) demands humility. We must consider others first. Next, Christian brotherhood demands loyalty. We must stand firm with our brothers and sisters. We do not always have to agree, but we need not publicly deface them either. A loyal brother or sister is one who remains and waits for the closed doors to engage in pertinent "family" discussions. Christ's brotherhood also demands passion. Our passions must align, and our north star, so to speak, is Christ himself. When our vision remains fixed on Christ, the need to confront or contradict a brother subsides because our passion for something greater than ourselves takes precedence.

Today's Prayer

Lord Jesus, teach me what it means to be the family of God. Chip away at my pride so that I may find true humility. Galvanize my loyalty to my brothers and sisters while you also infuse my passion for you with a holy encounter.

The Long Pause

The Long Pause" is here to remind you to take a break from the normal routine and reflect, not only on this longer piece, but also on your own life rhythms. What needs to change? What needs to stop? What do you need more of? Use this long form piece, along with the reflection questions, to enhance your daily times with God.

Christ, Our Delight

One summer during my undergrad years, I received private tutoring in Greek. I walked into Dr. Randolph's humble home and sat next to him at his computer. He set the font size at 300 percent. It was huge. His eyes failed him, but his mind was sharp as a razor.

Before we began our session he said, "Tim, do you know why we study the Greek language?"

"No," I said.

"We study the Greek because we love the Word."

I didn't reply. I just listened.

"We study the original language because we love the Word of God," he repeated.

I nodded, giving him my assent, and we began our session. We met only for a few sessions, and then I was off to the next thing. But that day, when I nodded, I lied. I didn't love the Word of God, and I knew it. I knew it as soon as he made the statement. I wanted to know for knowing's sake. How embarrassing.

Dr. Randolph passed away years ago. So many people grieved his death. He lived his life in love with the Word of God. This no one would dispute. I knew him before our session. But having personal interaction with him made his passing so much harder, especially since I came to him for "learning" when he wanted to fuel my passion for the Word.

I will never forget his statement.

In 2013 the History Channel ran a miniseries titled *The Bible*. I do not watch much television, but I watched this. Say what you want about this particular perspective of the biblical narrative, but I will tell you this: as I watched, I choked back tears almost the whole time. My wife noticed. She asked, "Why are you crying?"

All I could think about were Dr. Randolph's words: *"We study Greek because we love the Word of God. Do you love the Word of God, Tim?"*

As I stared at the screen, watching Abraham tie up Isaac, preparing to gut him for the sacrifice, my eyes filled up. When my wife asked me why I was crying, I could finally answer Dr. Randolph's question truthfully:

"Because I love the Word," I said to her.

She did not reply. We both kept watching.

John the Beloved wrote, "In the beginning was the Word, and the Word was with God, and the Word was God." When I replay Dr. Randolph's question to me, I hear this: "Tim, do you love Christ, the Son of the living God?"

And then I hear my response: "No, Dr. Randolph. I do not. I only want to know in order to fulfill my pride, to fulfill an obligation, to look smart around others. To be an intellectual snob."

Time has ticked on since then. And now I read the popular blogs and articles and commentary and cultural hoo-ha, and I wonder who among us loves the Word. Further, I wonder how many of us, in the name of biblical and intellectual snobbery, put on airs—cherry-picking the Word of God to satisfy our own prideful idolatry.

Do you love the Word? Is it living and breathing in your brain right now? Or do you crack your Bible only to know for knowing's sake or maybe only for selfish comfort?

The Word, the *logos,* shines as our north star in this life. But it's difficult to follow something we don't love. Do you love the Word of God? Do you love the Christ? King David wrote, "I will meditate on your precepts and fix my eyes on your ways. I will delight in your statutes; I will not forget your word" (Psalm 119:15–16).

Delight and God's Word too often seem at odds. We errantly view God's Word as cold dogma, a set of rules to be followed. But perhaps we should take another look at his Word. Perhaps we need to refresh our perspective by approaching Scripture as we would approach the relationships we love best—perhaps we should approach Scripture as Christ himself.

When we do, we see "your ways" not as taboos but as helpful signposts, directing our steps in a world and culture preoccupied with puffing up individuals. Christ's ways are, indeed, difficult at times. But he does not leave us alone as we pursue him. Rather, he reminds us that we are his friends, and friendship with the Divine shimmers as our most beloved relationship, comforting us in the midst of pain and disappointment.

Reflection

1. How do you view and use Scripture? Is the Bible a book you pick up once a week as you run out the door for church?

2. Do you struggle to dig into the Bible because of some past associations? Perhaps you grew up in a legalistic home where the Bible was used more like a baseball bat to correct immoral living than for a healing agent. If so, do you feel there is room for healing? Pray for that, and pray for Jesus to make his Word come alive for you. Remember, his Word is his communication to you; it is living and active. He wants to talk to you through his Word, so pray for that.

3. Keep in mind, however, this is not time to bash or unleash pent-up anger. Rather, it is a time to renew and refresh, to even obtain a whole new perspective on the Scriptures.

4. Practice breath prayer while reciting a short verse. A breath prayer is just a short, almost spontaneous prayer that you pray through the day. Some people use a different breath prayer every day; some use the same breath prayer for an entire week. Pick a short, familiar verse and pray that verse every day for the whole week. Perhaps it's a prayer of thanksgiving taken from the Psalms, or one of the Bible's poetic benedictions, such as, "The Lord bless you and keep you; the Lord make his face to shine upon you and be gracious to you; the Lord lift up his countenance upon you and give you peace" (Numbers 6:24–26). Use a verse like that as your weekly prayer. It will aid your reflection, it will inspire your memorization, and it will remind you of God's grace and provision for you.

Application

1. If you struggled through a legalistic upbringing—or if you can relate in a similar way—then find some time to write about your views and hang-ups related to the Bible.

2. What do you need to do to get past your spiritual baggage? Talk with your pastor, a friend, your spouse. Take time to wipe the slate clean between you and your past so that you can approach the *Logos* with new and fresh eyes. You can't hear God in his Word if you resent it.

3. Next, read through an entire book, like 1 John, in one sitting. Write down your thoughts on John's tone, why he seems to be writing, his passion, his view of Christ. As you read, pray about what you are reading and ask the Lord to give you fresh eyes, a fresh heart, and an excitement to get to know him again, for the first time.

4. Many people I know regard the Scriptures as dull or boring, and I certainly see that. It was like that for me for longer than I'd like to admit. But when I began reading the Bible with open ears—really listening for God to speak to me—then things changed. My heart felt open to his message, and I cared less about my own biases or past hang-ups with the Word. Staying in one book for an extended study helped me familiarize myself with one writer and that writer's message. This week, pick a New Testament book, not a Gospel but perhaps one of Paul's or John's letters. Read it through each day (well, one of Paul's shorter letters—not Romans!) and pray for God to reveal himself in the reading.

Identity

Threads of Fear and Wonder   DAY 1

I will praise You, for I am fearfully and wonderfully made. Marvelous are Your works, and that my soul knows very well.

Psalm 139:14 NKJV

On Tuesday night during nighty-night time, Lyric, my five-year-old daughter, asked, "Daddy, can we go up to God?
"Why do you want to go up to God?"
"I have to ask him something."
"Well, we can talk to God right here, right now."
You can imagine how the rest of the conversation proceeded. If Lyric had her druthers, she'd board her rocket ship and visit God daily just to talk with him. Discussions like this one occur about every five seconds when you have little ones. And I am always struck at the unique perspectives my girls possess.

When do we lose our unique perspectives?

In the cultural ocean of sameness, the only things that distinguish us are those unique qualities that make us, well, us.

But the temptation in our specialized culture of sameness is to drill down on our strengths. However, as my good friend Dr. Stephen Graves reminded me once, if you focus only on your strengths, you develop blind spots and become *one-dimensional*.

Developing core competencies is important. But we should never shelve things about ourselves simply because they appear either weak to the modern world or because they don't *fit* in traditional paradigms. Who wants to be one-dimensional, anyway? I like stick figures, but I don't want to *be* one.

Lyric's rocket ship perspective on communicating with God melts me—it makes her unique. It's not my job to instruct her on the postures of prayer. It's my job to learn from her uniqueness—a uniqueness, an identity, still untarnished by adult hang-ups.

You are not everyone else. You are you. For you were made in the secret place, woven together with threads of fear and wonder. God fashioned your physical body with special intent. He blew into you his own breath, quickening your innermost parts—your soul.

In the quiet of eternity God saw you—the you that is full of complexity, quirks, silliness, warmth, intellect, dreams, and giftings. Wherever you go, God is with you. Whatever you do, his sovereignty holds you.

Today and forever don't let anyone dictate your identity to you. Rather, with sweeping delight, let the light of your life so shine before the world. And lest you think I am bewitching you with self-help hoo-ha, think again. To understand your identity is to rest in confidence in the will of the Father for you.

Today's Prayer

Lord Jesus, guide us with your will. Help us be ourselves—fearful and wonderful children of the heavens!

Invade Me   DAY 2

> Jesus, knowing that the Father had given all things into his hands,
> and that he had come from God and was going back to God,
> rose from supper. He laid aside his outer garments, and taking
> a towel, tied it around his waist.
>
> John 13:3–4

In one of the more stunning scenes in the Gospels, Jesus stands up from the upper room table, disrobes, takes a basin of water, and begins to wash Peter's feet. Peter responds not with humility but with indignation: "You will never wash my feet!" His intentions are good, though steeped in the protocols of the culture—how often we miss what Jesus calls us to because we care too much about what culture thinks.

Jesus instructs Peter, "If I do not wash you, you have no part with me." Then the game changes for Peter, who now wants to be cleaned from head to foot, again missing the point. Jesus was showing Peter what it means to be a disciple, to be his friend. It wasn't the water on Peter's feet as much as it was Jesus on his knees.

Jesus invades us where our hearts are most reinforced by worldliness, and most of us at some point have pawned ourselves to the world.

The cultural expectation for success possesses great strength. It sways our hearts away from what Jesus really wants from us: a way in.

Today's Prayer

Lord Jesus, today I confess to you the arrogance of my strength. I do not want to pursue culture's lie anymore. I want to open up so that you can not only find a way in to my heart, but so that you can possess it completely.

The Support of My Father   DAY 3

Today's Prayer

Lord Jesus, you have given me the shield of your salvation,
and your right hand supported me,
and your gentleness made me great.
    You gave a wide place for my steps under me,
and my feet did not slip.

Psalm 18:35–36

A Vulnerable King   DAY 4

Then he poured water into a basin and began to wash the disciples' feet and to wipe them with the towel that was wrapped around him. He came to Simon Peter, who said to him, "Lord, do you wash my feet?" Jesus answered him, "What I am doing you do not understand now, but afterward you will understand."

John 13:5–7

Jesus wants a way into our hearts and minds. He wants to possess both. He showed us what it takes to be his friend. It takes vulnerability. To be vulnerable means to be open to attack, to let yourself out there, to kneel in front of someone willing to serve.

In essence, when Jesus knelt to wash Peter's feet, he was inviting Peter into community. Take a moment to reflect on the scene once more. Jesus kneels as a way to show Peter and the disciples what it means to be in community with him and the Father. You must let yourself be open to attack, be vulnerable, maintain a posture of perceived weakness from the world's standards. And that is just what Jesus is getting at—the world and its "way." He offers a different way: his. In fact he offers himself as the Way. Jesus wanted Peter to be in and remain in relationship with him. But to walk in Christ (i.e., to walk in the Way) is not merely to be accepted into a group. Like any thriving relationship, accountability is inherent. Jesus told the disciples to do for others what he had just done for them: kneeling, washing, serving. If we accept the friendship and intimacy of relationship that Christ offers, it comes with an element of accountability. I have loved you, he says, now go and love others, that's the deal.

Today's Prayer

Lord Jesus, I want to walk in your way. I want to walk in you. My heart is weak and does not trust so easily. I want to be intimate with you. Teach me to be open to attack—to be open to the attack of your love.

The Measure of You   DAY 5

If I then, your Lord and Teacher, have washed your feet, you also ought to wash one another's feet. For I have given you an example, that you also should do just as I have done to you. Truly, truly, I say to you, a servant is not greater than his master, nor is a messenger greater than the one who sent him. If you know these things, blessed are you if you do them.

John 13:14–17

This week we have looked at how unique we are to God. He made us as individuals with special qualities, and those qualities can help others if we remain confident in who we are in Christ. We've also learned what it means to be in communion with Jesus, to be accountable as we follow his model for loving others, and the importance of vulnerability in our relationships.

Identity consists of more than simply knowing who you are and what you're good at. Your identity also draws itself from those with whom you share community. We need not ask ourselves, "How am I known by others?" Rather, we should ask, "How deeply have I shared myself with others?"

Too often we judge ourselves by external markers. But we will only ever find our true selves when we are strong enough to be vulnerable, weak enough to let others in, and needful enough to account for the way in which we love and serve others.

My father has served as a pastor for nearly forty years. He told me that when you help others, all the worry in life dissipates. We spend too much time wrapped up in the anxieties of leadership and building our "identities." If we really want to find our selves, we will do so at the feet of others. This posture does not dismiss vision and ambition. Rather, it recalibrates them. We cannot cast vision and follow ambition when both rise from the heart of the world. For we can only rise when Christ raises us. We can only lead when we finally realize our need to follow.

Today's Prayer

Lord Jesus, I want to show others your way, not mine. Thank you for showing me how to find myself—by losing myself in you.

Dragons

My Dragon of Doubt DAY 1

But let him ask in faith, with no doubting, for the one who doubts
is like a wave of the sea that is driven and tossed by the wind.

James 1:6

At the beginning of anything "big" lies a dragon called Doubt.
She's sly, but she doesn't rely on cunning. She spans the
horizon, but she doesn't rely on her range. She relies on what
she knows—that her presence alone thwarts many who would
walk the path set before them.

My whole life I've wondered, *What does it mean to follow
Jesus?* I have no answers, only a life opening to the horizon of
doubt. *Can I really go this way, Lord? Won't I be eaten or pulverized or taken captive?* Always the answer is a hushed, "Follow me."

Today's Prayer

*Lord Jesus, I hear you whisper for me to follow, but what
about that dragon there? Can you help me past it? Can*

*you give me a sword? A magic ring? Bravery? Help my
doubt today, Lord.*

Faith, My Directive   DAY 2

And Jesus answered them, "Truly, I say to you, if you have faith
and do not doubt, you will not only do what has been done to
the fig tree, but even if you say to this mountain, 'Be taken up
and thrown into the sea,' it will happen."

Matthew 21:21

I have to assume that if my faith directs me, then it's taking me
to a heavenly place. And by that I don't mean some place in
the clouds—not right now, anyway—but it's a place he's been
before, or that he's seen and still sees—even now he is looking
at it. He is whispering to me all the way, "Follow me."

"Where, Jesus? Where are you? Where do I go?"

The dragon snarls and huffs. The horizon quivers. But the
whisper persists.

But I know where to go. My questions? Just stalling tactics.

I know the seed he's set within my heart. Not because I've
achieved any great spiritual thing, but because I've listened.
Blessing, it seems, comes from listening and then following
directions.

"Many live in obedience more from necessity than from love,"
wrote Thomas à Kempis in the *Imitation of Christ*. "Such become discontented and dejected on the slightest pretext; they
will never gain peace of mind unless they subject themselves
wholeheartedly for the love of God." Do I believe because I
should, because of necessity? Or because of love?

And so I continue to follow. Over the sheep of England,
around the double-decker buses on my mountain bike that sticks

out like a sore thumb in the land of 1950s' metal-fender cycles, I follow—my everyday a constant willful act of listening, then following—literally, one foot in front of the other. Or, in my case, one word after another, after another.

Today's Prayer

Lord Jesus, I don't want to follow you out of necessity. I want to follow you because my love and affection for you leave me with no other choice. I want to slay the dragon of doubt with my searing affection for you.

Eye of Faith   DAY 3

Today's Prayer

Lord Jesus, praise to you. The twisted oak, black against the white rollers of the morning sky, drips praise to you— the raindrops pelt it and roll off, dancing in the puddles below.

Praise to you, O Lord. You were Abraham's provider, and you continue with me, with us all.

Keep close to this reviving fire, and see if thy affections will not be warm. In thy want of love to God, lift up thy eye of faith to heaven, behold his beauty, contemplate his excellencies, and see whether his amiableness and perfect goodness will not ravish thy heart.[1]

Praise to you, O Lord. The fields roll on in emerald waves, their sheep spotting the highs and valley lows—the ridgeline stretches south and punctures the low-hanging rain clouds. I am showered in autumnal rain. I am showered in blessedness, in simple beauties green and gray, black and burnt orange.

Praise to you, O Lord, for the day unfolds and every square inch of it shouts for you. And I shout for you: Strengthen my faith, that I must trust you with finances. Strengthen my desire, that I may want you more, and more. Selah.

Strands of Love and Kindness · DAY 4

There is no room in love for fear. Well-formed love banishes fear.

1 John 4:18 THE MESSAGE

I know, Lord. I know. But I can't see that far. I know you hold it all, all of it. But I want to hold it before I believe it. Can I do that? Can I hold it first?

I know you're capable to supply the need. And I don't mind asking. But my belief wavers. My mind cries out and scrambles to the closest worldly anchor—well, for a time they feel like anchors, all those things I think I control. And when I consider this and that, I doubt, I doubt, I doubt—my direction, my calling. What if my faith veers me and I don't know it? What if my intentions, which I think true, are really clouded with pride?

O my God, why do I stumble over my own feet? Why do I foster a spirit of fear—the bedfellow of doubt? Where does fear fit in with my relationship with you?

Forgive my selfishness and worrying heart. Forgive my short-sightedness. Even though I stumble over my weak heart, I cannot fall far from your mercy. Your graciousness picks me up and I, once again, live.

Your words to Isaiah comfort me. Your arm is not too short to save. I create the barrier; I build the wall—my sin and me. I lose sight of your vision for me, how you desire my triumph. I sit making mud pies when the vineyard sprawls just beyond the bend. Why can't I see?

But you opened my eyes, O Lord! I see the veil hiding me from you. Of course you hear me. Of course you possess the strength to save. Your beauty, to me, is your steadfastness. You can't disown yourself. Even when I stammer in my faithlessness, you remain faithful.

And there you are, O Lord, my God, dressed in your armor: your breastplate of righteousness, helmet of salvation, garments of vengeance, your cloak of zeal. You come riding to me, to me! You come on the intensity of a flood that you cause with your breath!

You are my Warrior God. You shoot the shots of deliverance with strands of love and kindness following behind. You stoop to feed! I eat and I am filled. You bend to help, even when I can't help but wallow in my pride and doubt and muck.

Today's Prayer

Lord Jesus, reassure me somehow that the life I have now is only the beginning. I want to feel born again, to feel like I'm living![2]

The Beauty of Home   DAY 5

I've told you these things for a purpose: that my joy might be your joy, and your joy wholly mature. This is my command: Love one another the way I loved you. This is the very best way to love. Put your life on the line for your friends. You are my friends when you do the things I command you. I'm no longer calling you servants because servants don't understand what their master is thinking and planning. No, I've named you friends because I've let you in on everything I've heard from the Father.

John 15:11–15 The Message

Most weeks I cannot decipher the difference between Monday and Friday. The blur of it all looks the same; only what lies at the end of the day is different. On a Friday our bodies relax around 3 p.m. as we shut the day down, excited to "get home."

The American writer and theologian Frederich Buechner says, "The word *home* summons up a place . . . which you have rich and complex feelings about, a place where you feel, or did feel once, uniquely *at home*."[3] We long to arrive *at home*. A place of familiarity and of beauty, a beauty we take in through our pores, as Beuchner puts it. And yet it is not only a place—it is the people who complete our homes. They are final pieces of the puzzle.

Sometimes we need the beauty of familiarity, and that is enough to rest our minds and hearts from doubt. But complete rest comes from the beautiful ones in our lives, our families and friends. Christ did not have a place to lay his head; his *at home* was within the sweet gossamer confines of prayer, he along with the Father. It was also with his friends, the twelve men we refer to as his disciples. Jesus emphasized brotherly love when he called the disciples friends. He consummated the friendship by doing what John the Beloved reminds us to do in his Gospel: he gave his life up for his friends.

Being home looks a lot like beauty, but not only the pleasurable kind we see—the kind we experience through the actions of our loved ones. We can rest in this life knowing that friends love us, that family loves us, that Jesus calls us friends. Today I head home. I yearn for the encouragement gained from the beauty of home: the low lights of my study, the south wind blowing into my window, the loving arms of my family, and the safe haven of heavenly love.

Today's Prayer

Lord Jesus, I long for rest. I need time away from my dragons. The week has pummeled me, and my spirit pines for the comfort of you—the comfort of home.

Disappointment

My God, My God! Why? DAY 1

> From noon to three, the whole earth was dark. Around mid-afternoon Jesus groaned out of the depths, crying loudly, "Eli, Eli, lama sabachthani?" which means, "My God, my God, why have you abandoned me?"
>
> Matthew 27:46 THE MESSAGE

When I sat down to write, I scribbled a new character name into my Moleskine. His name is Avian. I sketched out his family, and before I knew it I was crafting his entire story.

When he was a young boy, Avian lived the life of privilege and honor that comes from being a prince. At twelve, he discovered he possessed a special gift. In the same year, his whole family was taken from him. He was left to believe they were all lost in an awful tragedy; only he was saved. His guardian took him far to the north—away from those who wanted to take his precious gift.

Over the years, he and his guardian settled in a quiet mountain town. In time, however, those seeking Avian's special gift discovered them. Now seventeen, Avian was forced to flee; his journey revealed more and more about his past and the secrets his family kept from him.

Lately he's been wrestling with a deep-seated betrayal. He hates that his family kept secrets from him. The same man who took his family now chases him far to the west, and all Avian can do is focus on what was taken from him. He doesn't eat much, just gnaws on revenge and bitterness. In one scene he loses control and descends into vengeance itself. There was nothing I could do other than let him ride off and kill a dragon.

Many of us deal with our past betrayals and disappointments daily. Those feelings we thought were buried deep rise most unexpectedly. When we let them linger, they turn us into something ugly. Our comfort? Christ was abandoned in his moment of greatest need. He *became* ugliness so we could live in beauty. He *became* the pathway out of our pasts and into *his* future.

Today's Prayer

Lord Jesus, grant us the life of the cross so that we may possess the power to choose to live not in our disappointments and betrayals, but in your pathway of victory and truth. Lord, I take comfort in the fact that you were betrayed by the very people you came to save. I know you feel what I am feeling today. I'm tired of living in disappointment. I want to move into your comfort, your peace. Move me, Lord Jesus.

Hang Your Burden Upon the Willows   DAY 2

Come to me, all of you who are weary and carry heavy burdens, and I will give you rest.

Matthew 11:28 NLT

Consider Psalm 137. It is a poem of lament. It is vivid and strange and sad. This image stuck with me: *By the waters of Babylon, there we sat down and wept, when we remembered Zion. On the willows there we hung up our lyres.*

These people were captives in a strange land. They could not sing, only contemplate revenge. When Avian (the character I told you about yesterday) snapped, he was eating lunch beneath a great hemlock in the mountains. Avian was in a strange land. But instead of finding a way out, he went farther in.

Today, perhaps you need to hang up your lyre on the willow branches and lament a little. Maybe you feel yourself tumbling further into the pain you can't seem to let go of. Maybe, like these Israelites, you've returned to a "land" that is shattered and destroyed. Maybe today you need to kill a dragon. Maybe today you need to let God play for you and sing you back into his love.

Today's Prayer

Lord Jesus, I seek your rest, not because I am running in this life, but because I am lifting burdens and dragging sorrow. I crave your rest.

Lift Up My Soul, O Lord!   DAY 3

Today's Prayer

Lord Jesus, to you I lift my soul. In you, O God, I place my trust. Do not let me be put to shame! Do not let my enemies triumph over me!

Today seems too much for my narrow shoulders. I cannot bear the weight of shame, of guilt and despair. My responses to those whom I love flare out of my despair and cast ugly shadows.

But your brilliance cannot be overwhelmed, this I know. And yet, even though I know this to be true, I cannot help myself—I dive into the bitterness so easy to access, so readily available and fed by the bent culture in which I live. It encourages me to focus on me. It tells me to consume and possess all that I can, all my greedy eyes think will satisfy.

It instructs me in the ways of the sensual and profane. It convinces me of their benefits and cloaks them in cultural snobbery—persisting in the lie that they will make me feel better, look better, talk better. To be versed in the culturally acceptable will make me feel better about my despair. It will keep the disappointment at bay and wash over the gouge left by betrayal.

Let it not be! Take the lies far from me and dump them into the icy northern sea. Your truth eclipses the shadowy rhetoric of culture and engulfs the lies, the profane and sensual. These, to you, are bent images of what you created. And it is the bent things, offered by the Enemy, that I run to so often to feel better. But refreshment, I know, can only come in the cool peace of your salvation.

In my salvation I have hope. For in salvation you give unlimited peace. You give yourself, unlimited and free. You lift me up and fill my soul with this goodness—a goodness no disappointment can overwhelm. For light pushes the shadows. The dawn brings the new day, and I find your compassions new again. I am flooded in your faithfulness.

Stay Vigilant   DAY 4

Delight yourself in the Lord. . . .
Psalm 37:4

Disappointment does its best to drag its victims into the ground. It is not subtle in its intentions. "Comfort!" we cry. And we run to everything and everyone but God. Finally, we find wisdom and cling to the cross. But too often disappointment has completed its mission.

Hell rejoices when God's children fall along the path. What could be better than to seed discouragement and bitterness, darkling elements into a Child of Light? The Enemy wants you and me to become less and less, but not in the sense that John the Baptizer meant it. Rather, to become less and less our selves—less and less of the way God created us. Our delights originate with God, and when they remain pure, the Child of Light thrives in delight, spreading brilliance to everyone.

"The deepest likings and impulses of any man are the raw material," says the old devil Screwtape to the apprentice devil Wormwood as he tries to turn the believer away from God, "the starting-point, with which the Enemy has furnished him. To get him away from those is therefore always a point gained; even in things indifferent it is always desirable to substitute the standards of the World, or convention, or fashion, for a human's own real likings or dislikings."[1]

You and I possess such tremendous power within our delights. But it is a power easily dimmed by hard circumstances. When disappointment moves in, it tends to linger, and there is nothing more coarse and ugly as a Child of Light banging around in the shadows, bruising others because he or she cannot shake the bitterness.

Today's Prayer

Lord Jesus, keep the light of delight ignited within my spirit. Protect me from the subtlety of disappointment. Stay ever by my side as I walk through this life, as I confront an enemy bent on removing me from delivering your brilliance to a darkling world.

Victory   DAY 5

Why are you depressed, O my soul? Why are you upset? Wait
for God! For I will again give thanks to my God for his saving
intervention.

Psalm 42:5 NET

Victory does not always feel like soaring. At times it feels
like digging—digging your way out from the rubbish heap
of disappointment. Other times it feels like pushing—pushing
through the lingering bitterness. And still other times it feels
like smashing—smashing the mirrored glass of disillusionment.

I am digging today. I am pushing today. I am smashing today.

For you did not make me to wallow, but to rise. And I rise on
the wings of your glory, your grace, your strength.

Today's Prayer

*Lord Jesus, you give me the strength I need to overcome
the negative thoughts conceived by disappointment. Be
my sweetest thought.*

Shame

Known DAY 1

My sheep hear my voice, and I know them, and they follow me.

John 10:27

Where did shame go? We live in a society where authenticity means to share everything, all our dark secrets, and all things we wish someone knew about us. We applaud such authenticity and call each other brave when we share or blog about something that we have kept in the shadows.

I love authenticity. I love it because it champions the truth about a person. But sometimes I wonder if we have allowed ourselves to play into the *spirit of the culture,* exchanging discernment for license. No shame, no holds barred, no distinction between sacred and profane.

The push for authenticity stems from our innate desire to be known. Brennan Manning says, "God calls me by name, and I do not answer because I do not know my name."[1] Though we are hardwired to be social, to want to share, to want others to know us, we struggle to find peace in who we are in Christ. We want so badly to express our brokenness in an effort to connect, to relate, so we feel less alone.

Of course, our desire to be known is not wrong, only at times misplaced. It is when we finally come to terms with our selves in Christ that the desire for naked authenticity finds satisfaction.

Today's Prayer

Lord Jesus, I desire to be known by you. I want to recognize your voice, and I want to know the name by which you call me. I am yours, Lord Jesus.

Who Will Satisfy?   DAY 2

Come, see a man who told me all that I ever did. Can this be the Christ?

John 4:29

W hen the woman at the well ran into Jesus, he asked for something to drink. She struggled to understand why a Jew would ask a Samaritan woman for water, but Jesus turned the conversation around on her and said, "If you knew the gift of God, and who it is that is saying to you, 'Give me a drink,' you would have asked him, and he would have given you living water" (John 4:10).

She tells Jesus he has nothing with which to draw from the well because it's deep. Then Jesus tells her that if you drink from this well, you'll still thirst. But the water he offers comes from a well of eternal life—all-satisfying. The woman presses Jesus for this living water.

Then Jesus tells her all she ever did. She was astonished he knew so much about her: about her past marriages and her current living arrangement (living with a man who was not her husband). We don't know too much of her past, other than she might have been living in shame—due to being dependent on someone not her husband, due to abandonment, we don't really know.

What we do know, however, is the woman realized she'd been seeking something or someone to satisfy her and found this very person in Jesus, the one person who shows he knows her inside and out. "This story is not about immorality; it's about identity."[2]

Today's Prayer

Lord Jesus, in you alone do I put my trust, for you alone can satisfy. I stand upon the rock when I find my identity in you.

I Am   DAY 3

Today's Prayer

Lord Jesus, I consider you now, in the quiet of the morning, and pray with desperate whispers—I want to hear you. I want to know my own name. I am scared of you, at times, and drift into the comfort of the less threatening and the more accommodating. Like the woman at the well, I want you to look deep into my life, my past and my future. I want you to tell me everything I ever did because I want to be known by you.

Now, exhausted from the day, from the week, I lie upon my bed and wonder: Who am I that you should know me? My days fall apart so often. My attitude crumbles because of my impatience. I find myself angry at myself and pray that you can still know me.

Look past the weak me and into the I AM in me. You are, Lord Jesus, beneath me, before me, and all around me. But right now, I just want you to know me.

Shame Drives Us to Christ   DAY 4

Jesus said to her, "Everyone who drinks of this water will be thirsty again, but whoever drinks of the water that I will give him will never be thirsty again. The water that I will give him will become in him a spring of water welling up to eternal life."

John 4:13–14

Jesus did not condemn the woman at the well for her past mistakes or unfortunate circumstances. Instead, he offered her himself. He offered her a safe place where she could be known. Her shame dissipated as she ran from the well and told everyone she'd met a man who knew everything about her. What acceptance! What peace!

Sometimes our desire to be known gets the best of us and we jettison shame and discernment so we can fling ourselves into the world, hoping someone will identify. Ravi Zacharias says secularism has created a culture where there's no distinction between what should be viewed and used as profane and what is viewed and used as sacred. He says, "Show me . . . a culture without shame and I will show you a monstrosity in its making."[3]

I believe, as Christians, our collective lack of shame comes from our individual desire to be known. The irony being, Christ calls each of us by name and invites us into an intimate relationship with him, and yet we ourselves do not know our names.

What would happen if we reveled in our known-ness in Christ and told others about the One who knows us through and through?

Today's Prayer

Lord Jesus, you search me, you know me. When I sit and when I rise, you know my thoughts deep inside. I want to find rest and peace in my known-ness with you.

Cheap Frankness   DAY 5

If you cling to your life, you will lose it; but if you give up your life for me, you will find it.

Matthew 10:39 NLT

If you read C. S. Lewis's collection of essays *God in the Dock*, you'll find his final interview conducted in 1963 at Magdalene College, Cambridge University, with Sherwood Wirt from the Billy Graham Association. Mr. Wirt asked Lewis if the modern use of the profane within writing as a means to make writing seem more authentic is necessary.

"I do not," said Lewis. "I treat this development as a symptom, a sign of a culture that has lost its faith. Moral collapse follows upon spiritual collapse. I look upon the immediate future with great apprehension."

Mr. Wirt followed up Lewis's response by asking if the culture has been de-Christianized. Rather than commenting on the greater culture, Lewis looked directly at the church.

"I have some definite views about the de-Christianizing of the church," said Lewis. "I believe that there are many accommodating preachers, and too many practitioners in the church who are not believers. Jesus Christ did not say 'Go into all the world and tell the world that it is quite right.' The gospel is something completely different. In fact, it is directly opposed to the world."

I find Lewis's ideas on accommodation, spiritual collapse, and feigned authenticity poignant even now, over fifty years later. We live in the age of the marketing-savvy provocateur pastor, the liberated speech of the blogosphere, and the land where the obscene and profane point to shame and mock.

As Lewis wrote, "The 'frankness' of people sunk below shame is a very cheap frankness."[4]

Perhaps most surprising is our general lack of humility. Here I take Richard Foster's definition of humility as being aware of the truth of things: I am aware of the truth of others and myself and of the situation in which I find myself.[5]

Humility demands we understand our position before God. Without him we are raging rebels bent on destroying. *With* him we become like Christ himself—the archetype of the humble servant.

We seem to forget who we are, or worse, we fabricate a humility and authenticity by way of our crassness and snark, writing it off to the gods of the hip and the real. And in the midst of our forgetfulness we ramshackle shame and stand blind to the notion and importance of hiddenness.

Part of our awareness of self lies not in our pathological need to expose everything in our lives in the name of "being brave" and "getting it all out," but in the realization that shame helps us see ourselves as we truly are. It helps us stay humble.

"When men attempt to be Christians without this preliminary consciousness of sin," writes Lewis in *The Problem of Pain*, "the result is almost bound to be a certain resentment against God as to one who is always making impossible demands and always inexplicably angry."[6]

Lewis does not claim to be a "worm theologian." On the contrary, he does not even believe in total depravity. He does not think we should be afraid of our true selves. He suggests that in order to know our true selves, we must learn through the lens of shame and right position before God.

The Altar of Self promoted by our culture looks inviting. It says that shame is a dangerous game—liberate yourself and find your true voice.

But Christ's message is something completely different. He says, "If you lose your life, you will find it." Perhaps it is time we return to lostness—a lostness in him, and in so doing, finding the trueness of ourselves.

Today's Prayer

Lord Jesus, I want to find myself, but I do not want to do it without shame. I want to learn humility from you. Help me stay low to earth, and in my lowliness find wings through your grace and the beautiful way that you know me.

Strength

You Are Brave   DAY 1

> I have told you all this so that you may have peace in me. Here on earth you will have many trials and sorrows. But take heart, because I have overcome the world.
>
> John 16:33 NLT

What does it mean to be brave? Allow me again to utilize Avian, a character in my fiction writing whose journey takes him from innocence to loss to revenge to the nothingness inherent in vengeance. At his lowest point, a friend tells him that in order to overcome a mounting evil he must become brave.

But he doesn't know how to be brave. He knows how to be brash. He knows how to let his emotions rule his actions. He knows how to use people for his own gain. He even learns how to kill. But killing and all the rest leave him in a dark place, alone.

Avian discovers that in order to truly conquer, he must not overcome the opposition. He must overcome himself.

Today's Prayer

Lord Jesus, teach me to be brave. I know you have gone before me. I know that no matter what circumstance I encounter in life, no matter what mountain I must climb even today, you have already overcome. But the biggest mountain I must overcome is myself. Teach me your ways, O Lord, that I might understand what it means to die to self.

The Emptying of Trust   DAY 2

Therefore, since we are surrounded by so great a cloud of witnesses, let us also lay aside every weight, and sin which clings so closely, and let us run with endurance the race that is set before us, looking to Jesus, the founder and perfecter of our faith, who for the joy that was set before him endured the cross, despising the shame, and is seated at the right hand of the throne of God.

Hebrews 12:1–2

I find that when I work through what it means to trust God, I have to move past the anxious thoughts and notions swimming in my brain. It's a place beyond me. A place like that looks different from my petty desires. Once I arrive at that place of trust, I act. But action isn't always indicative of a trusting heart.

How many of us work, work, work, so we can live safe and secure? We cover our bases like the Israelites who "trusted" and prayed to God, but also prayed to the foreign gods of the earth just in case. After all, a little prayer to the god of rain can't hurt when you're a farmer. A little sacrifice to the god of money can't hurt when your mortgage is due.

A *true* act of trust, however, looks different from our own fumblings for security and gain. It looks like sacrifice.

Back to Avian. In one scene, Queen Faylinn, Avian's mother, helps him grasp a hidden and special magic. "My children," she says, "I want to tell you a secret. There is another kind of magic. It is a magic that springs forth from hope itself and is found in the most innocent of things within this realm. Few people know of it, and those who do, fear it. For its power is very great. It reaches into your heart when you use it, and it will try to hold the very things you love and hold most dear. No kind of badness can stand against it. Only those brave enough to hope will ever have a chance to experience it. And only the chosen can wield it. You carry magic within you, Aviar, this you know. And I wonder and wish, my runes rise to hope, that perhaps you are the brave one among us. That maybe your hope is stronger than all our fears. That your heart is pure enough to find its magic."

"Momma, how do I be brave?" asked Avian.

"To be brave, you must become invisible to yourself."

In the first century, to become a Christian meant to court martyrdom. The book of Hebrews describes the faithful early Christians who were sawn in two and ripped apart, and yet their faith wavered not. These Christians trusted and acted, and their actions revealed their hearts' position: in the hand of God. They lived invisible to themselves.

Faith demands invisibility of self.

Today's Prayer

Lord Jesus, I want to be invisible to myself. I want my acts of trust to show my true heart. My heart is yours.

Straining Toward Christ   DAY 3

Today's Prayer

Lord Jesus, I have obtained nothing, nor am I already perfect, but I press on to make your resurrection my own, because you have made me your own. Forgetting what lies behind and straining forward to what lies ahead, I press on toward the goal for the prize of your upward call.

For you, Lord Jesus, shine as my guiding light. You help me keep perspective and understand your ways. I realize that in order to rise I must first go down into the darkness, only to emerge, baptized by your holiness, your humility, and grace. Shower me, Lord. Grow me in your perfect light.

The Brave Among Us   DAY 4

If we say we have fellowship with him while we walk in darkness, we lie and do not practice the truth.

1 John 1:6

As we consider the early believers and their willingness to sacrifice all for their faith, we must ask ourselves how our spiritual bravery compares these twenty centuries later in the post-everything world. Between our (Christian against Christian) social media fights and theological arrogance, our thirst for provocation, and the endless cause-based hills to die upon, where have all the brave Christians gone?

In *The Cost of Discipleship*, Bonhoeffer asks, "How then do the disciples differ from the heathen?" He answers by saying that Christians should go beyond what is expected in society to what Bonhoeffer refers to as *extraordinary* living. If society values self-promotion, the Christian should work to promote others. "The better righteousness . . ." he continues, "must have a motive which lies beyond itself. Of course it has to be visible, but they must take care that it does not become visible simply for the sake of becoming visible."[1]

The family of God (the church) must find a better way. Not to *be* better, but to become more like Christ. We must point to the extraordinary by following the most extraordinary Way. But we can't do this when we're bent on being brash and manipulative, governed by sinful emotions, and killing within our hearts.

Following Jesus leaves insecurity and our vengeful hearts behind. It demands an act of trust and another act of trust, and another. We wake into trust. We sleep, trusting. We serve, because we trust. We sacrifice because we trust. We become invisible to ourselves. We become brave.

Today's Prayer

Lord Jesus, help me to find the better way in this life. I know that it is you and your Way, but my own pride keeps me from your path. Take my insecurities and replace them with trust. Help me to be extraordinary for you.

Strident   DAY 5

He's right there with you. He won't let you down; he won't leave you.

Deuteronomy 31:6 THE MESSAGE

Travelers grow weary, and we are all of us travelers. Our paths cross and intermingle and yet remain unique in direction. We can relate to one another. We *should* encourage one another.

Our culture likes to critique. Christians like to follow suit. But the words that drip from our lips should be wine to those who need refreshment and honey for those who need revival. We should stride with one another, barking courage into the hearts of our brothers and sisters.

"Be strong. Take courage," I say, "Don't be intimidated. Don't give them a second thought because God, your God, is striding ahead of you. He's right there with you. He won't let you down; he won't leave you."[2]

God himself strides with you!

"I won't give up on you; I won't leave you," he says. "Strength! Courage! . . . Give it everything you have, heart and soul. . . . Don't get off track, either left or right, so as to make sure you get to where you're going. And don't for a minute let this book of the Revelation be out of mind. Ponder and meditate on it day and night, making sure you practice everything written in it. Then you'll get where you're going; then you'll succeed. Haven't I commanded you? Strength! Courage! Don't be timid; don't get discouraged. God, your God, is with you every step you take."[3]

And so we travel on, through the lay-offs, through the disappointments, through the loss, through the betrayals, through the grit of it all. For we will not be overcome—Jesus himself is the Overcomer!

"I love the man that can smile in trouble," wrote Thomas Paine, "that can gather strength from distress, and row brave by reflection. 'Tis the business of little minds to shrink; but he whose heart is firm, and whose conscience approves his conduct, will pursue his principles unto death."[4]

Be brave. Be brave.

Today's Prayer

Lord Jesus, help me row bravely today along with my brothers and sisters. I know you are with me—and so, peace goes with me. I am brave.

Passion

We Clack Before God

Blessed is the man who remains steadfast under trial, for when he has stood the test he will receive the crown of life, which God has promised to those who love him.

James 1 12

In the fall I seldom think about the naked branches beneath the turning leaves. But eventually, and almost without my noticing, all the leaves will be gone (some still cling), decomposing into the soil.

And there they are—the denuded branches, stiff and clacking in the cold. This process of dying finds us all.

So winter comes, and not without our complaints (except for those of us who love the snow and fires, like me). This week I've been looking past the leaves and into their winter, into my winter. What is my winter?

Does winter equal personal pain? Breaking relationships; fear of the unknown; stresses of parenting; rage birthed by an undisciplined attitude? I think winter *can* symbolize pain.

But winter's death is much more than the bleak times of life.

Winter moves in rhythm with the earth. The earth moves to the rhythm of God. Our hemisphere tilts away from the sun, the air clears, a more complete light blasts through our atmosphere, the sunsets blaze and the sunrises vault, though the sun itself bends solstice low. In winter, nature sleeps, driven into itself by the cold. Roots reach while snow and ice enchant the gray ridgelines.

The rhythm of the human winter mysteriously heals and deepens *us*; it strips us of our veneers so that we can stand and clack before God—the true us. We dive into the dark, hard soil of life; in cold corners we cower. We walk out into elements unkind. But walking does not end winter; no amount of hope can. Winter must pass, for it has its time.

Brothers and sisters, pull tight the pea coat, blanket, or cowl, and walk into the cold. Though God allows grief, he does not afflict from his heart. Remember, though, the progression—the cross comes before resurrection. And so winter must pass. Remember too that his compassions are new each day. And this alone strengthens our stride.

One foot . . . in front . . . of the other. Step, again. Now, once more. Walk, clack, repeat.

Today's Prayer

Lord Jesus, thank you for strengthening me to endure this winter.

The Power of Winter   DAY 2

I did not go up to Jerusalem to see those who were apostles before I was, but I went into Arabia. Later I returned to Damascus. Then after three years, I went up to Jerusalem to get acquainted with Cephas and stayed with him fifteen days. I saw none of the other apostles—only James, the Lord's brother.

Galatians 1:17–19 NIV

Passion is stoked by the fires of time and commitment. When Paul converted to Christianity, he went into the wilderness. He took three years to learn and to pray and to listen. It did not hamper his passion for his newfound Savior. Rather, it galvanized it. Reflect on this short segment from Richard Foster on the value of winter within the spiritual life. Read Galatians 1 and consider how Paul's example can teach you as you continue through life, desiring more of God but not always finding the passion you thought was yours to obtain.

Foster writes, "Winter preserves and strengthens a tree. Rather than expending its strength on the exterior surface, its sap is forced deeper and deeper into its interior depth. In winter a tougher, more resilient life is firmly established. Winter is necessary for the tree to survive and flourish. . . .

"So often we hide our true condition with the surface virtues of pious activity, but, once the leaves of our frantic pace drop away, the transforming power of a wintry spirituality can have effect."[1]

Today's Prayer
Lord Jesus, teach me the value of spiritual winter.

Take Off Your Sandals DAY 3

Today's Prayer
Lord Jesus, "Do not come any closer," you said, "Take off your sandals, for the place where you are standing is

holy ground."² *But I did not realize where I was standing; I failed to recognize your holiness. Am I washed up in my spirit that I cannot feel, sense, hear you? Then you told me your name: "I am the God of your father, the God of Abraham, the God of Isaac and the God of Jacob."*

Instantly, I was afraid. I could not look at you, but you picked me up and showed me the way to passion—passion for life, passion for my family, and passion for you. For they are all wrapped in one: you. Thank you, Lord, for showing me how to burn for you.

God Interruptions DAY 4

Don't fret or worry. Instead of worrying, pray. Let petitions and praises shape your worries into prayers, letting God know your concerns. Before you know it, a sense of God's wholeness, everything coming together for good, will come and settle you down. It's wonderful what happens when Christ displaces worry at the center of your life.

Philippians 4:6–7 THE MESSAGE

When you wake each morning, what thoughts instantly press into your mind? How did *this* morning find you? The first things of the morning that alight upon our minds will either drift us through our day in a hazy clamoring of more, more, more, or they will point us toward the brilliance of God himself.

A few nights ago a powerful storm swept through our town. I woke to the constant sheeting of rain and house-rumbling thunder. Moments later I heard my two-year-old cry out. I entered her room to find her and her older sister, Lyric, awake. Lyric was trying to console Brielle, to no avail.

Brielle eventually calmed and fell asleep, so I lay with Lyric. She was intent on listening to the storm.

"Do you want to go downstairs with me?" I asked.

"Yes, Daddy."

We walked downstairs and I opened the front door. Her eyes widened. The lightning illuminated the swaying oak and birch branches. I held her on our tree-stump bench under the porch. She could not stop "Oooing" and "Ahhing" with each thunder-clap and lightning flash. It was a 3 a.m. memory-making time—just a giddy four-year-old and me praising the midnight storm.

The morning came fast; my eyes sagged like wet sheets on a wash line. But my first thought? *Thank you, God, for my storm time with Lyric.*

My mind had run with anxious thoughts before I went to bed, but those thoughts were interrupted by the storm. I needed that interruption. I needed some awe to overwhelm my anxiety.

When we fail to plan daily awe-interruptions, the business of life will take over. If we are not careful, we will find ourselves waking with work and planning top of mind, instead of grati-tude or a hunger for more of God. Anxieties tend to rule the day, but we can quell them if we remember to allow the beauty of God's interruptions to change the course of our hearts.

Midnight storms may not always help us wake in the right frame of mind, but we can create a life rhythm that *includes* God interruptions.

Today's Prayer

Lord Jesus, wake afresh with me. Rain down upon my mind. Wipe away the residue of my anxious yesterday. I don't want daily anxieties to keep me from giving you thanks.

Feeling Dead   DAY 5

My soul is in deep anguish. How long, Lord, how long?

Psalm 6:3 NIV

Can you really hear me today, Lord? The rain drives, not only drenching the fields, but flooding my heart with weariness and sorrow. My heart wastes away. Turn, Lord, and deliver me; save me because of your unfailing love. All night long I flood my bed with weeping, and drench my couch with tears. My eyes grow weak with sorrow.[3] Where is my passion? Where is my life?

But then you come. I lift up my voice in quiet prayer and you say, "Grief and days of rain will come, my son. But my love endures, because I am love and I AM that I AM. I extend into eternity, spanning your future and past. I hold it all, but more important, I hold you today. In my eternality you will find singularity—a universal yet unique love just for you. Passion for me will wane, but it will also be the thing that keeps you above the crashing whitecaps. I am coming to you soon, take heart and rise above."

Today's Prayer
Lord Jesus, thank you for lifting me up—for your grace even when the fervor in my heart wanes.

Calling

Stuck in Words

Sovereign Lord, you are God! Your covenant is trustworthy, and you have promised these good things to your servant.

2 Samuel 7:28 NIV

What is *calling*? Am I called to be a dad? Am I called to be a schoolteacher? I cannot remember the first time I ran into the concept of calling, but I remember my response: "Calling? What's that?"

The good ol' American pragmatism kicks in quickly with this concept. In the United States, the name of the game is efficiency. Or is it solutions? Or maybe the name of the game is win? Everyone wants to know the sensible way. How do I fix my career? In order to get a job, what must I study? What must I do?

Less focus is given to reflection; still less is given to prayer. And what does it mean to listen? I interviewed pastor and author Francis Chan once. I asked him what he thought about calling. He said instead of calling, he would rather discuss obedience.

In order to obey, we first need to listen. Saul's failure to listen to God led to his subsequent expulsion from the crown of Israel.

You and I are called by God to be his ambassadors in this world. Inherent in our faith is the call to follow Christ, to be like him in how he lived his life. This is the general calling of the Christian. Our jobs and careers don't always connect to a specific vocation. I am a writer, and I will always be a writer no matter what career path I choose. If I decide to pursue real estate as a career, I don't cease to be a writer. A friend of mind says calling is where your vocation and career meet.

That's a fine definition, but today's thought is not about defining *calling* so that you and I can find the right job. Rather, today our goal is to listen to God and to discern direction from his leading.

Today's Prayer

Lord Jesus, this week, as I begin to reflect and pray about calling, help me to understand that I am really reflecting on how I do or do not trust you. Grow my trust, Lord!

I Am Listening   DAY 2

Thomas said, "Master, we have no idea where you're going. How do you expect us to know the road?"

John 14:5 THE MESSAGE

Today I woke up. The wind sounded like it was using a stick to beat my window. The sound hammered on the glass and subsided. I walked bleary-eyed to the kitchen to start the tea. I was surrounded. The wind came from all sides—a harrowing attack upon the house.

With tea in hand, I found my study chair and sipped while the wind tried to pry open the window. I watched the trees heave back and forth. The clouds did not hover in a static pose. They tumbled over the blue, while the morning sun lit them from the east—a dazzling display of movement, sound, and emotion.

I listened. I watched. I breathed deep.

Sometimes God's voice raps upon our hearts like the wind on my window. He wants so badly to direct us, and yet we refuse him—as if opening the window would allow the wind to draw me up into the sky. God's wind-voice calls to us, but we seldom listen, because it usually calls us to an ocean we must walk across—and we'd rather not. Not, first, without getting that bonus, or great job, or stability we so desire, that we think will afford us the flexibility and bandwidth to do all those things the wind is telling us to do.

We don't really listen to God. We acknowledge his existence and nod to him from church. But that voice echoes through the windows of our lives; we do not possess the time or energy for such a task. That would be imprudent.

Today's Prayer

Lord Jesus, I admit, I'm not really listening to you. I am safe in my house and you are beating at my window—and I sit, afraid to venture out there where the clouds catch fire and roll into the great conflagration of tomorrow. I want to listen. Help me listen.

The Hum of Nothing   DAY 3

Today's Prayer

Lord Jesus, I hear a hum. It comes from inside of me. It sounds like a violinist bowing one string, constantly, over and over, the same string. I do not fear the hum. Indeed,

I am transfixed by it. Is that you, Jesus, humming in my head? Is that you, bringing your sound into my life?

Before today I did not hear. I would not hear. Today, though, is different. My ear bends to you, O Christ. I can hear you—there you are, on the cross. I hear you breathing; it's staggered and labored. I can hear your skin stretch and give forth blood. I hear you exhale and end it all. I hear the sky rage and turn black. I hear you, O Christ.

Your death sings to me today. It calls to me. In my selfish humanness I feign questioning: What is it that God wants of me? What is my true calling? I am not fulfilled; what must I do to find fulfillment? And then I remember the sound of your breathing—the sound of your blood pooling at the foot of the cross. And then I hear you say, "I want you to follow me."

"But Lord," I say. "I cannot follow you. I do not wish to die. I cannot take the pain."

"I will shoulder your load. I will carry your burden. I will consume your pain. Only follow me. Do you hear me? Are you listening?"

"Yes, I do—I am. Help me, my Christ."

What More?   DAY 4

Do not let your hearts be troubled. Trust in God, and trust also in me.

John 14:1 NLT

What more do you want from me, Lord Jesus? Can you not see? I am neck-deep in this mess at work, at school, at home. Why do you pester me with this, this thing? I can feel it pressing into my brain—or is it my heart? I think I know what it is you want me to do. But the timing is not right. I have too much at stake.

My schooling.

My career.

My kids.

My work.

Too much; just too much. I have to steward all of this well, right? You will hold me accountable, so I must do this well. But there is always this pulling. I cannot escape the pulling.

Is this my calling? Is this my chance to obey? All these games I play with my mind, trying to discern your voice from crazy. Are you crazy, God? Because if your idea fails, then what?

Do we trust God enough to say yes? Have we only said yes to ourselves up to this point? Yes to all the appropriate and sound opportunities afforded us?

Today's Prayer

Lord Jesus, I want to hear your voice even clearer. I know it is you, but I am too weak today to follow. I cannot obey. Have mercy on me! Help me to obey. Help me to not only hear, but listen.

The Road   DAY 5

Jesus said, "I am the Road, also the Truth, also the Life. No one gets to the Father apart from me."

John 14:6 THE MESSAGE

How long must we spend with Jesus to really get it? Thomas spent three years with Jesus and still did not get it. He wanted to follow Jesus but did not know the way. Or perhaps he was looking at it all wrong. Maybe he was expecting Jesus to lead the disciples in a more political fashion. What was the strategy? How would they go about it? Where is that you're going, Jesus, and how will we follow you?

Following is about trusting. If we do not take the step we know God is telling us to take, then we should consider the depth of our trust. When you and I trust a person, it shows in our actions. As children on the playground test trust by falling backward into their friends' arms, so too do we as adults test trust by how much we tell, how much we give, how much we release.

The same is true with regard to our trust for God. His voice and leading can come to us in many ways: circumstances, insight through his Word, dreams, the exhortations of friends. But even though we say we know and understand how he speaks, we still linger, reluctant to move from our place of familiarity. We trust ourselves, and that's really the truth of it.

If, however, we desire to follow Jesus, to walk in him, then we need to trust him.

Today's Prayer

Lord Jesus, why is it so hard to trust? We humans are weak-minded, frail-hearted. My desire is to follow, but my fear tells me not to trust. Have grace, Lord. Help me see even just a glimpse of you in the fog of reality blinding my vision of the heavenly plan. I will follow, I will. But I need grace today. Help me trust.

Beauty

The Beauty of Witness

> If any of you is embarrassed with me and the way I'm leading you, know that the Son of Man will be far more embarrassed with you when he arrives in all his splendor in company with the Father and the holy angels.
>
> Luke 9:26 THE MESSAGE

I often revisit the early church document that follows. It inspires my own witness. It challenges my behavior within the community of believers, but more so in the public square. Pray through the text and weigh your own witness. Ask yourself, "Am I the soul of the world?"

For the Christians cannot be distinguished from the rest of the human race by country or language or customs. They do not live in cities of their own; they do not use a peculiar form of speech; they do not follow an eccentric manner of life. This doctrine of theirs has not been discovered by the ingenuity or deep thought of inquisitive men, nor do they put forward a merely human teaching, as some people do. Yet, although they live in Greek and barbarian cities alike, as each man's lot has been cast, and follow the customs of the country in clothing and food and other matters of daily living, at the same time they give proof of the remarkable and admittedly extraordinary constitution of their own commonwealth.

They live in their own countries, but only as aliens. They have a share in every thing as citizens, and endure everything as foreigners. Every foreign land is their fatherland, and yet for them every fatherland is a foreign land. They marry, like every one else, and they beget children, but they do not cast out their offspring. They share their board with each other, but not their marriage bed.

It is true that they are "in the flesh," but they do not live "according to the flesh." They busy themselves on earth, but their citizenship is in heaven. They obey the established laws, but in their own lives they go far beyond what the laws require. They love all men, and by all men are persecuted. They are unknown, and still they are condemned; they are put to death, and yet they are brought to life. They are poor, and yet they make many rich; they are completely destitute, and yet they enjoy complete abundance. They are dishonored, and in their very dishonor are glorified; they are defamed, and are vindicated. They are reviled, and yet they bless; when they are affronted, they still pay due respect.

When they do good, they are punished as evildoers; undergoing punishment, they rejoice because they are brought to life. They are treated by the Jews as foreigners and enemies, and are hunted down by the Greeks; and all the time those who hate them find it impossible to justify their enmity. To put it simply: What the soul is in the body, that Christians are in the world.[1]

Today's Prayer

Lord Jesus, empower my witness with your spirit. I want the world to see you in me. I want them to say of your glory, and me: "This person is part of the very soul of the world."

The Beauty of Obedience DAY 2

And Samuel said, "Has the Lord as great delight in burnt offerings and sacrifices, as in obeying the voice of the Lord? Behold, to obey is better than sacrifice, and to listen than the fat of rams."

1 Samuel 15:22

Consider the words of Oswald Chambers on the topic of obedience:

My personal life may be crowded with small, petty happenings, altogether insignificant, but if I obey Jesus Christ in the seemingly random circumstances of life, they become pinholes through which I see the face of God. Then, when I stand face to face with God, I will discover that through my obedience thousands were blessed. When God's redemption brings a human soul to the point of obedience, it always produces. If I obey Jesus Christ, the redemption of God will flow through me to the lives of others, because behind the deed of obedience is the reality of Almighty God.[2]

In the Samuel passage, Saul pleads his case and defends his actions. He was God's chosen king, and God instructed him to destroy the Amalekites, even the livestock. But Saul kept some of the spoils from the battle and then lied to Samuel about it. Perhaps Saul thought he could talk his way out of it. After all, in the ancient Near East it was assumed that obedience in the temple courts meant sacrifice of some kind was involved. Maybe Saul felt he could cover his actions with a "Well, I was just keeping some things to make a good sacrifice to God" type of excuse.

Saul should have known. God wanted him to listen and do, but he did not listen. He did what he wanted to do, what was right in his own eyes, and he lost his throne because of it.

Oswald Chambers points to the fruit of obedience; when we listen to God, good things come of it. When we do not listen, only bad ensues, and that is the beauty of obedience—the fruit of the redeemed looks like heavenly blessing.

Today's Prayer

Lord Jesus, I hear you telling me to do _____. To be honest with you, it sounds a little crazy. I cannot see the good that will come of it. I cannot even see past the instructions, and yet you call me forth. What is keeping me locked in this place of indecision and even rebellion? Shake me from my complacency, O God! I want to do this thing, but I do not understand. Help my understanding, and help me to listen and do.

The Beauty of You   DAY 3

Today's Prayer

Lord Jesus, hear my prayer. Today I am focusing on your beauty. Thanksgiving falls from my lips when I consider the beam of your glory, within which my life stands. I do not even remember the world without your color bleeding all over my eyes.

The storm passes and I shudder at the glimpse of your back. The finch dips and bobs in the winter oak at midnight, and the eerie glory fills me—even in the dead of night the birds of the air sing your praise. The actions of my daughters, my wife—they possess an element that staggers me, that leaves me without speech, just quiet heaves of thanksgiving.

The sight, the experience, affects me. I sense you, and my knowing grows. I know you, and my feeling intensifies. You are awful and good, tremendous and raging—you, the holy hurricane spinning within the world. You quicken the dying and breathe a hush into the winter pines. "Crawl into me," you whisper to me as I walk this path in the evening twilight. Purple, blue, and orange—you inhabit, you create, I sing, I dance, I shout, on.

First Things   DAY 4

Ah, Sovereign Lord, you have made the heavens and the earth by your great power and outstretched arm. Nothing is too hard for you.

Jeremiah 32:17 NIV

We live in the land of the pragmatist. Our culture is results-oriented. We "get things done!" Hand in hand with pragmatism is the rational. We think, we do, we succeed. In Christian apologetics especially I see this. We usually dig our line of defense along rational lines, vying for truth against the New Atheism or postmodern subjectivism.

Of course we need to think with soundness of thought, and we should be able to defend the Christian faith when answers are demanded of us. But I wonder if answers solely based on rationality are really what the world seeks.

Today I want you to reflect on the Sovereign God who made the heavens and the earth; how he created, what he created, and who he created. I want you to meditate on the beauty of this planet, the beauty of your family and friends, and the beauty of God himself. What if we, instead of pointing out all the places where an absolute must be, pointed to something else entirely?

In the preface of *The Great Divorce*, C. S. Lewis mentions the idea of a supposal—a fictional creation on his part that sets the stage for a possible scenario about reality and then asks the reader to simply consider. Lewis was a master at creating the supposal. Aslan himself is one giant supposal. Suppose a guardian type of being exists in this real world similar to the big lion in the Narnia world—that would explain this sense of wonder and fear and awe that I receive when I encounter something good, or a sunset, or a thriving relationship.

And so, today, consider beauty. Suppose we began to paint our Christian apologetic in a different light. Suppose we began to point folks to beauty—beauty in our lives, in our relationships, in nature, in reconciliation, in all of it. Perhaps in using beauty as apologetic, the rough edges of our sophisticated Christianity would fall off. And we can all do with a little bit of smoothing out in that area.

Today's Prayer

Lord Jesus, I am drawn to your creative wonder and to the beauty of your being—your love and grace and mercy, all so beautiful. Help me to show the world the beauty side of my faith, along with the rational side.

Lost in You   DAY 5

Like the appearance of a rainbow in the clouds on a rainy day, so was the radiance around him. This was the appearance of the likeness of the glory of the Lord. When I saw it, I fell facedown, and I heard the voice of one speaking.

Ezekiel 1:28 NIV

In one sense, we are never lost if we find life in Christ. In another sense, once we enter into relationship with him, we fall into an abyss—the eternal falling into love and glory. It does not end, this falling.

When I entered into marriage, I was eager to journey with my wife. The excitement of discovering more about her intrigued me. Certainly there would be an end to the "knowing" process, but as it turns out, the longer we journey in our relationship, the more we uncover, the more we stumble, the more we climb to new heights.

You and I reflect God. We carry his image, which is an immense theological topic. But today, as I think about being lost in the relationship with my wife, I see the eternality of God within it. My relationship with my wife helps me understand how to deal with a quiet God, a forceful God, a giving God, a loving God, a God who will stand by me no matter what.

If I am brave enough to enter into this relationship with my wife, why do I so often hesitate to get lost in God?

Today's Prayer

Lord Jesus, the beauty of you is that you never end. Your glory touches and envelops everything. I want to get lost in you. I want your glory to drip into my life the further into you I journey.

Eclipse

It Is Finished

O death, where is thy sting? O grave, where is thy victory?

1 Corinthians 15:55 KJV

Where would you be on Sunday if you lost your oldest son in a car accident on Saturday? Not in church. At least, I don't think I'd be in church.

Last Saturday I received an email from my pastor explaining that a seventeen-year-old young man from our church was tragically killed in a car accident.

His parents are godly, joyful, and passionate for Christ's kingdom, dedicated to their children, and pursue Christ with every ounce of their being. Tom Robertson serves as one of our elders. Katherine serves at being awesome. Early Saturday they received the most grievous news a couple can bear. They lost their oldest son.

I expected the congregation to fill the church on Sunday. I was not disappointed. When I walked in, my friends Dave, Mandy, and Brian were already pouring out their hearts to God, leading the family of God in praise, worship, and mourning. The Spirit of God was so thick in the room, I gasped.

After the music ended and Jon, our pastor, took the stage, my wife tugged my arm.

"They're here."

"What?" I whispered.

"The Robertsons are *here* . . . in church." I looked at Chris and she pointed to my left about three rows up. Sure enough, there they sat—stretching the length of a whole row. The held each other, wept, listened, and worshiped.

Following a bold and victorious message about pain and parenthood and sovereignty, Brian and Mandy led us in another song. The Spirit tugged me up to the front row. I stood by my pastor and we wept and praised God. The music continued, the congregation dismissed, and I stood praying for the Robertsons. When I opened my eyes and turned, Tom motioned me to him. I climbed over chairs, walked over the rows, and bear-hugged him. I prayed for him in his ear, "Lord, strengthen my brother. Strengthen him."

And then I heard Jesus speak to me . . . through Tom. In my ear Tom replied, "He has. He is. I'm great. I'm so great."

The congregation collapsed on Tom and Katherine and the kids. Tears and laughter and weeping—all the sounds of the family of God loving one another.

I arrived at church hoping to *be* an encouragement. I left church encouraged by a father and mother who were hours away from the epitome of pain. And then I heard Jesus again.

"Where, O death, is your sting?" I could hear Jesus shouting it to me. And his voice echoed into the caverns of my heart, then up into the clouds. "Where are you, you death?"

Again the voice came, "It is finished! It is finished! You have no power over my children."

I gripped the wheel and shook.

Today's Prayer

Lord Jesus, we remember those who've lost family members and we see how you comfort people with a deepness unknown, a deepness that comes from the Holy Spirit. And, Lord, we hear your voice! We rest and live in the peace and anticipation that you—you, YHWH!—conquered death and hades, and you return for us! Come Lord Jesus, come. Dona nobis pacem. *So be it, amen.*

Home With You   DAY 2

He will wipe away every tear from their eyes, and death shall be no more, neither shall there be mourning, nor crying, nor pain anymore, for the former things have passed away.

Revelation 21:4

Our time on this earth is not guaranteed. My friends lost their son without notice, and by all counts, entirely too soon. But even now as I reflect on the brevity of life, my heart looks into the future in an effort to grasp the meaning of it all: life, death, and everything in between. Society churns with play, school, and business, and it all feels so big when we live inside of it, the everydayness at times overwhelming our brittle hearts.

But, as overwhelming as it seems, God weaves hope with the promise of Christ's return—the return of the King. Imagining a time of no more tears and no more mourning can provide a salve for our dear losses. But then there's the getting up and putting on our shirt and pants and shoes; there is the continuation of life, and verses about a future salvation from pain do not always cut it. We still ache even though we know what is coming.

Perhaps this verse from Revelation provides us with something else that we often miss, for it comes at a climactic moment in the passage. It is not merely the act of Christ wiping away our tears. It is the fact of coming home. Finally, at the end of it all we will be with him, with the King. It is the reconciliation of humanity with God and a reinstatement of our intimacy with God—like a new garden of Eden. We will be with him.

In this lies our peace. When we look at our temporary pain through the human lens of suffering, we find ourselves overwhelmed. But when I realize that I will finally be home with my heavenly Father, then I no longer look to just the wiping away of my tears; I look to the fulfillment of everything my heart desires. When we find ourselves back home with Christ, we have no need of desire or comfort, because he will fulfill it all. This is my hope in time of pain. This is what I look toward as I continue on in the everydayness. I work, I play, I love, I live—all to glorify him, yes, but all to find my way back to him as well.

Today's Prayer

Lord Jesus, you are my home. Today my breath prayer is about "home." Home, with you. Help me in my day to glorify you, to bring help and healing to a land hurting and in need of you. I live for you, and I live so that I can once again be with you.

The Eclipse of Glory   DAY 3

Today's Prayer

Lord Jesus,
Be thou the well by which I lie and rest:
Be thou my tree of life, my garden ground;

Be thou my home, my fire, my chamber blest,
My book of wisdom, loved of all the best;
O, be my friend, each day still new found,
As the eternal days and nights go round!
Nay, nay—thou art my God, in whom all loves are
bound![1]

Caught in His Hurricane   DAY 4

> So we have come to know and to believe the love that God has
> for us. God is love, and whoever abides in love abides in God,
> and God abides in him.
>
> 1 John 4:16

In the popular worship song "How He Loves," the lyrics talk about how our human affliction is eclipsed by God's glory. We are like trees bending beneath the hurricane winds of God's mercy and grace. Today, God's wings of love overshadow your afflictions.

And do not think for a moment your afflictions amount to nothing. An affliction does not have to be catastrophic to be real and serious. God affirms you in your affliction and understands that this world hurls blackness at you in the form of broken relationships, shattered marriages, ruined careers, parenting slip-ups, failure at school, loneliness, despair, feelings of worthlessness, and the list goes on.

What the worship song does so well is reiterate the absolute love God has for his children. Today remember his love—his deep Calvary-love for you, his child.

Today's Prayer

Lord Jesus, today I feel bent down, low, and brutalized by the afflictions this world is so good at hurling at me. I know Paul says our afflictions are light and momentary in light of your eternal love. Please, Lord, bring your eternal love to me today in a very real way. I want to see your glory. I need to feel you today. I need your hurricane-love.

Knowing God's Love   DAY 5

In this the love of God was made manifest among us, that God sent his only Son into the world, so that we might live through him.

1 John 4:9

The word *love* receives its fair share of interpretation in our culture. The Christian understands love as originating in God himself. This love came to live among us in Christ Jesus. His life, then, offers us a template for living in love, though we often distort it with our own perspectives.

Theologians tell us that God loves not because we, the perceived objects of his love, are worthy of love, but because God is, himself, the essence of love. It is not that God is loving, but that his nature is love itself. And so he must love—he cannot help himself.

God's love is not some fuzzy affection in the way we humans so often perceive love. God loves us in order that we might live.

Think about the ultimate illustration of love—Jesus, God's one-of-a-kind Son, dying for the whole of humanity. What do we take from that sacrifice? That we too should sacrifice for one another. Yes, that is part of it, but only part.

We love because Christ loved. This is not saying that we should sacrifice because Christ sacrificed himself. It is saying that we should love because now we are truly alive. Because now it is in our nature to love. We have become like Christ, and Christ himself is love. We love not because we find people worth loving, but because we cannot help ourselves. If we do not love, then we are liars and the love of God is not in us. Strong words from John the Beloved.

Today's reflection is an important one. You set out this morning to learn something more of God through Christ Jesus. You know that the greatest act of love is to lay your life down for your brother. But twenty-first-century Christians rarely have this opportunity. How do we apply this kind of sacrificial love to our everyday lives?

Well, perhaps we are asking the wrong question. Perhaps the question about love we should be asking of ourselves is, Has my nature changed to be like Christ's? Do I love because I can't help it? The community to which John the Beloved was writing had to deal with leaders who were not loving people, who clearly needed help. The conclusion to this type of behavior is that these leaders actually did not know God at all. Their nature had not changed.

Our aim is that we love like God loved. He sent his Son to die for us. Christ gave up his life so that we might have life. When this kind of love marks our life, God's love finds perfection, or reaches its aim. An unbelievable thought: We can actually live in the perfection of God's love.

Today's Prayer

Lord Jesus, I desire to be like you in that I want to love like you love. I want my whole being to change, to be wrapped up in love. I want you to mark me, and I want my love to be your love. But I can only accomplish this through your strength, through your sacrifice. Give me the strength to die, to myself and for others.

Anticipation

Heavenly Vision

I will rouse your sons, O Zion, against your sons, Greece, and
make you like a warrior's sword.

Zechariah 9:13 NIV

How we love taking credit for our accomplishments, often
forgetting we are servants of the King. This is no lowly
worm-theology statement, however—serving the King of Glory
is blessed and full of purpose.

But it is rather easy to begin our days only considering what
we need to accomplish, what goal we need to achieve. In our
pursuit of excellence (which itself can often be misguided), we
find the end result simply too great to resist. Our progress equals
better this, better that, better me, better you. Accolades, accolades, accolades.

And in this frame of mind, the Christmas season can become
somewhat of a ritual in the most materialistic and negative sense.

We look forward to the gathering of friends, the music productions, and the lights and eggnog, the trees and gifts.

But what about our longing for the One who comes to set our hearts ablaze, to fight for us, to comfort us, to carry us upon his horse of peace and show us a new vision for the world—a heavenly vision? We need always remember that what we accomplish comes from God, and the way we remember is to keep heavenly vision.

Today's Prayer

Lord Jesus, I seek a new vision of the world today. Give me your eyes, your heart.

Salvation From the King Who Was Saved DAY 2

> Then the Lord will appear over them; his arrow will flash like lightning.
>
> Zechariah 9:14 NIV

Yesterday we began reflecting in chapter nine of Zechariah. We did not get far when we realized the importance of possessing God's vision, that it is God who accomplishes for us. It is too easy to take credit for success, especially in a culture that champions that way of thinking.

Today we find cause for praise, for Zion's King comes! And though he comes cloaked in humility and peace, he finds betrayal and death. "Behold, your king is coming to you; righteous and having salvation is he, humble and mounted on a donkey," writes the prophet Zechariah (9:9).

But the hope in this passage isn't that he brings salvation ("having salvation" is a poor translation, according to scholars), but that he himself experiences salvation from his heavenly

Father—YHWH. Even Christ himself will call out to God, and God will fight for his Son. We see this at Calvary. Though God turns his back, he turns to lift his Son from the depths.

God establishes the rule of Christ to the ends of the earth. If he does that for his Son, imagine what he will also do for you and me, heirs to the throne of glory!

In this Zechariah passage, God keeps saying, "I will . . ." I will: take away the chariots, free your prisoners, restore twice as much, bend Judah, bend my bow, rouse your sons.

O children of Zion, God himself bends his bow to make his children like a warrior's sword. And we see him do this with the Son, the Christ, who defeats death with death itself!

Today's Prayer

Lord Jesus, I am overwhelmed at how you fight for me. Thank you for your care and provision, and how you hold me when I cannot stand.

Only Through God Do We Prosper   DAY 3

Today's Prayer

Lord Jesus, today you are my fighter! You are my hope! You stretch out your hand to uphold me in times of distress! You prosper me!

You say to me, "I will restore twice as much to you" (Zechariah 9:12 NIV).

Let me not forget today that in my well-devised plans, it is you who supplies victory. I am your jewel in the land. I sparkle, like jewels on a crown (v. 16). How beautiful I am to you (v. 17). I am your sheep, and you care for me. Why do I toil in distress and worry, in anxiety and fear?

Today, Lord Jesus, I rest in the prayer of "I will, I will, I will." I praise you as I encounter the real of the everyday, as I discover that by releasing the thirst for accomplishment I allow a new thirst to surface—a thirst for Fire.

The Comfort of Sanctus   DAY 4

> Holy, holy, holy is the Lord God Almighty, who was, and is, and is to come.
>
> Revelation 4:8–9 NIV

There's a refrain I love to listen to as I enter into a time of prayer. It's called "Sanctus," the prelude to the German Catholic Mass, also known as the Prayer of Thanksgiving. The lyrics are simple:

> Holy, holy, holy Lord God of hosts.
> The heavens and earth are full of your glory.
> Hosanna in the highest.
> Blessed is the one who comes in the name of the Lord.
> Hosanna in the highest.

It contains two expressions of Deity. The first expression references God's transcendence as the awe-inspiring God of heaven. The second expression references the humble and indwelling divinity of Jesus the Messiah, God's immanence.[1]

What mystery, that the God of heavenly glory (transcendence) would come and walk among us (immanence). Reflect on this reality today. What does it mean to you to encounter God, both his transcendence and immanence?

Today's Prayer

Lord Jesus, this morning I lift you up in praise, Lord God of Hosts, that you would fill this day with the fullness of your glory. Grant me, Lord, an even more intimate relationship with you. Help me understand how your holiness fills each day with "otherness," with a sense that everything beautiful I see finds its origin in you. And help me also to understand the friend I have in you—you who came riding on a donkey and its foal—Immanuel, God with us. God with me. May the God of heaven and earth, the blessed Savior and the Holy Spirit, mark my life today.

Seizing Forever   DAY 5

And the world is passing away along with its desires, but whoever does the will of God abides forever.

1 John 2:17

The world is passing away. When I envision what John is saying here, I picture the world existing in the waning shadows of an autumn afternoon. As the sun falls, shadows lengthen and pass over the landscape. Yet at the same time the sunlight takes on an otherworldly look, beaming with a scintillating crispness that lures one away from the task at hand and out into a field, chasing the fading autumn brilliance.

So a simultaneous dying of the day along with the richest and most alive light of the day show us the mystery of a gospel that illumines and quickens even when the darkest shadows of life run deep on the landscape of our souls.

It is the act of chasing brilliance that keeps hope alive within our hearts. And that chasing act produces an expectation of belief—that though the shadows lengthen and at times over-whelm, the brilliance is not far away.

We live in the shadowlands. But we only know we live there due to the pushing of brilliance across the land. For where there is shadow, there is light, and where there is light, hope shines.

When I watch my girls play in the waning autumn sun, moving in and out of the oak shadows strewn across the backyard, I see the gospel. I see the magic and heavenly ability to move from shadow to light, shadow to light without any permanent soul damage. The girls will lay their heads down when the sun goes down and will rise to the brilliance spilling into their window.

The world is passing. And yet the gospel gives us the opportunity to rise into its brilliance. This is what John means when he talks about abiding in God and seizing forever. We wait as the shadows pass, abiding, waiting on the hope that comes from the Brilliance. Waiting on God.

Here's to the beauty of autumn's shadows and the everlasting hope of the pushing Brilliance that keeps us in the forever of tomorrow.

Today's Prayer

Lord Jesus, thank you for your brilliance; how it restores and renews even when the world crumbles around me. Let your gospel fill my today as I lift up others in your love. Keep the fire stoked within me as I look forward to your coming glory—to be united with my Lover in holy ecstasy.

Heights

On the Heights

He made my feet like the feet of a deer and set me secure on the heights.

Psalm 18:33

During my doctoral studies in England, some friends invited us to their home in the Lake District. One afternoon, just before sunset, I set out on a hike into the countryside overlooking Lake Windermere. As I walked, I could feel the pressure from my studies and our recent transition as a family of five moving from Atlanta, Georgia, to England. I was tired, but the November air refreshed me and drew me further up and further in, to use one of my favorite Lewis lines.

I followed the footpath along the stone fences, past a mountain stream and up onto a massive clearing with open views of the entire lake and surrounding villages. Sheep dotted the emerald fields, and the wind now ripped and pulled at my coat. Breathless, I sat upon an outcropping of moss-covered limestone boulders—the sheep carried on with their chewing and baying as if I were invisible.

I repeated Psalm 18:33 over and over in my head. I know the meaning of the metaphor teaches us about the provision and watchful care of a God who secures our footing when everything seems to be falling apart. But then, there on those boulders, the view, the wind, the sheep, the cold, I felt something more.

My hike took me high up into the mountainside. Already the sun had tucked itself behind the far western horizon. And still, I sat and listened. The elemental sound of wind across high grass was all I could hear—utter quiet. A kind of silence devoid of man-made sound. I found myself surrounded by raw nature, by a raw God.

Today's Prayer

Lord Jesus, you set my feet upon the heights—yes, to secure me. But Lord, there you are, massive and comforting. Keep me in your presence today, my Savior.

Surefooted   DAY 2

He gives me the agility of a deer; he enables me to negotiate the rugged terrain.

2 Samuel 22:34 NET

The wind from the mountainside spoke to me by way of comfort and refreshment. And as I sat upon the boulders, I wondered more about the mystery of the heights. The sheep walked and grazed, at home in this habitat of quiet and extreme height. But it took me several moments to stop fidgeting, to listen, to remain, to still myself.

There is a *mysterium tremendum* about the heights, unsettling and clarifying. God uses heights to show us his provision and care. But the heights also exude a solitude untouched by man—a holy of holies, if you will.

I find myself, now returned from the mountains of the lakes, looking for "the heights" in other places: a walk down the lane, a midnight stroll with my headlamp under the stars, sitting in the quiet of the nearby cathedral. They do not compare to the actual heights at the lake, but they instill in my mind, body, and soul a reverent quiet oft forgot in this age of noise and bustle.

Today's Prayer

Lord Jesus, I need thee, O I need thee. Take me to your heights and feed me your quiet and your reverence.

My Refuge   DAY 3

Today's Prayer

Lord Jesus, I hear, and my body trembles;
my lips quiver at the sound;
rottenness enters into my bones;
my legs tremble beneath me.
Yet I will quietly wait for the day of trouble
to come upon people who invade us.
Though the fig tree should not blossom,
nor fruit be on the vines,
the produce of the olive fail
and the fields yield no food,
the flock be cut off from the fold
and there be no herd in the stalls,
yet I will rejoice in the Lord;

I will take joy in the God of my salvation.
God, the Lord, is my strength;
he makes my feet like the deer's;
he makes me tread on my high places.
Habakkuk 3:16–19

The Vine Fails   DAY 4

Though the fig tree should not blossom,
nor fruit be on the vines,
the produce of the olive fail.

Habakkuk 3:17

The beauty in the prophet Habakkuk's words stem from his own certainty. How incredible that though the visible things of the world upon which we rely fail, the prophet lifts up praise. And how quick we are to crumble when we fail to gain acceptance into a certain college, or our career skids, or our relationship falters, or our marriage falls to pieces.

How much import do you and I place on the things we see in this life—the things by which we maintain our healthy and rich lives?

The big word in this verse is *though*. The preceding verses reveal a world of expectations falling apart, the glory of God invoking fear, and yet when the sources of sustenance wither, faith abounds.

Is your vine withering? Is your faith along with it?

Today's Prayer

Lord Jesus, I confess that my faith relies not on your sustenance and provision but on my own. When things go bad, my faith withers. Forgive me.

292

In the Basement DAY 5

His splendor covered the heavens,
and the earth was full of his praise.
His brightness was like the light;
rays flashed from his hand;
and there he veiled his power.

Habakkuk 3:3–4

Consider your God. He is called YHWH—a name the Hebrews would not even say because of its sheer holiness. Consider his splendor, how the prophet describes it covering the sky. The earth resounds with sounds of praise for him; think of the birds, the whales, the ocean crashing into the shore—all praise, all for him.

Consider his way. It is the way of light. If we walk in him, we walk in heavenly light. If we walk in heavenly light, we live within his might and power. He is so great, he shields us from seeing his fullness.

And yet, we linger in the betweenness. We tolerate the dimness of decay, preferring shadows to light. Søren Kierkegaard says every human being, if seen through the metaphorical lens of a house, has a basement, a first floor, and a second floor. But every human being enigmatically remains contented to live in the basement. "This is the building," writes the Danish philosopher, "but he prefers living in the basement, that is, in the categories of sensation. . . . He not only prefers living in the basement—no, he loves it so much that he is indignant if anyone suggests he occupy the fine suite lying vacant for him."[1]

Where are you sitting today? Does a suite await you, and yet you linger in the basement of sensuality, given over to the lusts of the world? What place have they in the Christian's life at all? Do you sit making mud pies in mud puddles unaware of the glory just over the hill?

I believe we hobble our own faith by basement living. We make and eat mud pies when a shimmering way of life extends before us. But we live lazy lives. Just over the hill is much too far. The heights? You cannot be serious. They are, well, too high—and what does one do up there in the wind and the quiet, anyway?

Have we truly exchanged God and his glory for the basement mud of our own filth?

Today's Prayer

Lord Jesus, I confess, I do not live on the heights. In fact, I would rather you not set me upon the heights. Forgive me for this attitude and strengthen my faith that I may, indeed, live with you—on the heights.

The Long Pause

The Long Pause" is here to remind you to take a break from the normal routine and reflect, not only on this longer piece, but also on your own life rhythms. What needs to change? What needs to stop? What do you need more of? Use this long form piece, along with the reflection questions, to enhance your daily times with God.

The Color Green

My heart weighs heavy as of late with the state of Christianity. I've spoken with dear friends who share similar sentiments, burdened with the lack of solidarity on the Internet and in politics, and the general lack of spiritual affection for Christ as well.

Where has Jesus gone in our thirst to build platforms, businesses, and wealth, and accumulate all the trappings of material success? Where is passion for Christ in the modern, sophisticated Christianity?

I'm not sure I know the answer to the pending question. I only know and am responsible for promoting unity in the space

I'm given to steward. I only know and am responsible for the spiritual affections in my own heart, first.

And yet, I find a war in my spirit. I want to bash heads together and pull us together in a massive prayer and worship gathering. But I also find myself wanting to head up to Mount Sinai alone and seek God's glory.

For it was only when Moses returned after a prolonged time alone with God that his face shone with a brilliance and pervading mystery. I find myself wondering, *What would it look like if my life shone like that, if my intimacy with God was almost tangible and visible to a world searching for something deeper than the next big consumptive purchase?*

Last night I listened to Rich Mullins's song, "The Color Green." Rich sings, "On my way to early meeting, I heard the rocks crying out, 'Be praised for all your tenderness by these works of your hands. . . . '"[1]

I was taken straightaway into a place like Sinai, or so it felt to me. And I could sense the Georgia storm clouds mounting a column of praise and the walnuts and oaks clapping in the storm breeze. "If no one will praise him, WE WILL!" they seemed to be shouting.

And I found myself praising and singing along with them in my Subaru. I was lost in the color green—for even the colors will cry out in praise. All the earth resounds, even if we won't, even we can only muster a halfhearted mumble—a tepid thanksgiving—through our grogginess, blank minds, and bland spirits.

By God's grace, I don't want my body and soul to wither like this. I want others to draw near to Christ, not my political view, not my stance on a social issue.

I want to wash in the blue of the sky and the green of the cornfields and the gold of the wheat. I want to fly in my spirit like the wrens, dart to and fro in avian dance like the American goldfinch. I want my life to clap like the oak leaves, praising and worshiping and serving with all that I have, all that I am.

"If they kept quiet, the stones would do it for them, shouting praise" (Luke 19:40 THE MESSAGE).

Reflection

1. Passion cannot be generated in mass group settings. Corporate worship allows us to come together as a family and worship, and certainly the dynamic of the masses and music and praise stokes the spiritual fire. But each person must cultivate a passion that maintains its blaze. Do you rely on group dynamics to stoke your personal fire?

2. Our passion for Christ looks and works like our passion for one another. We spend time with those we love. We sacrifice for our closest friends. We talk, discuss, fight, and forgive with our friends and family. Now we must reflect on our heavenly relationship. Is your heavenly relationship healthy? Are you even on speaking terms with God today, this week, this month?

3. Do the same qualities in your earthly relationships cross over to your life with Christ? Do you talk to him through daily prayer—prayer-like breathing? If not, how can you expect to maintain spiritual fervor? Do you allow cultural activities to push your time with Christ to the margins?

4. Take serious time to evaluate your spiritual passion. Have you become too accustomed to the world to realize that you are barely breathing spiritually? It is time for each Christian to get honest and kick spiritual nonchalance and mediocrity out of the spiritual house.

Application

1. Reflect on the year so far. Has something replaced your passion for Christ? Has work infringed on your earthly and heavenly relationships? Has school sidetracked you

into personal ambition? Get out your prayer journal or whatever you've been using all year and spend some time *writing* your end-of-the-year reflections. Mark the ups and downs of your spiritual life. Describe the sweetest moments with God. It doesn't have to be a novel, just write: "That one Sunday in June was the high point of my year spiritually. I'd like to get that back." That's it. Now pray it.

2. In these weeks, take some walks. Get outside and reflect on everything God has done this year. How has he provided? Thank him for provision. How has he blessed? Thank him for your blessings. How has he challenged you? Thank him for building you through trial.

3. Invite some of your closest friends over for a bonfire. Trust me, even if it's cold outside, it will be fun and you will be blessed. Provide beverages and some snacks and ask everyone to share how they've grown and how they've been challenged this year. It may sound intrusive or odd, but I've been doing this more and more, and I find that my closest friends love sharing where they are spiritually and love hearing where I am as well. This kind of communication does wonders for the heart; it encourages and sharpens. After you do it, email me about your experience. I can't wait to hear!

4. Now, get ready for Christmas. And do so not by running yourself ragged with all the hubbub. Rather, take time to strip away the unneeded fat from your life both physically and spiritually. Get rid of junk around the house; give unused clothing to your local clothing bank. Evaluate your television consumption, or maybe even get rid of your television.

   Clean out your email and work on de-cluttering everything. Ask yourself hard questions like, "How do I really use my time? Where do I spend my money?" These two questions will reveal truths you may not be comfortable with.

When I moved my family from Atlanta to Oxford, England, my wife and I asked these questions and were surprised at how much of both time and money we waste on frivolous things. We de-cluttered, sold things, and determined to live differently. We found our faith rekindled and God's voice louder than ever in our lives. I will promise you this: When you and I take steps to really hear God, we will find his voice ever present and realize that throughout the year he never moved—he never stopped talking, never stopped pursuing. It was I who moved away. Start fresh at the bonfire and give it all to him, again, for another year.

Jesus

Glory Invasion DAY 1

> Then the angel said to them, "Do not be afraid, for behold, I
> bring you good tidings of great joy which will be to all people.
> For there is born to you this day in the city of David a Savior,
> who is Christ the Lord."
>
> Luke 2:10–11 NKJV

Do you hear what I hear, ringing through the sky? A song, a song ringing through the trees, with a voice as big as the sea."

This Christmas carol is a song of hope resounding, hope wrapped in wonder—the immensity of Divinity alighting to the earth, to our hearts. It haunts and proclaims in whispers a goodness not unlike pure light.

It carries weight, this light of hope, and bears down upon the conscience of the world, drawing hearts unto itself. The invasion of such a glory, stretching the finite into a working kingdom of light; shards splintering into our everyday.

"Do you hear what I hear, ringing through the sky?" It fills up the firmament, pressing out the air with holiness, so much so that our vision blurs for the tears at beholding the ranging stars. How they glimmer to the sound, to the song, to the ringing.

I am so aware of you, O God, as I crunch the frozen tufts beneath my feet. Each step echoes in the great hall of your kingdom—a kingdom not of this world, yet throughout its very foundations and structures. I inhale and tremble, for you are my breath. I gaze above and quake, for the heavens drip you into my mind's eye.

I throw up my arms in surrender, for fear of my life! Have I not beheld the glory of the Lord? Has he not unveiled himself before me? Woe is me! I am utterly undone and forever damned!

But what is this I find, a child with a sword, an infant dipped in blood, the horses of heaven delivering him from the very depths of the *sanctus tremendum*—the tremendous shaking place of the Holy? Who is this I find, a ragged man, healer, and friend of the poor? Who is this I find, the vagabond wanderer of heaven, crying for me in a garden? Who is this I find, a friend and confidant, the interrupter of my death sentence? Who is this I find, the slaughtered Lamb, the one screaming for me though iron and wood splintering his flesh?

"Do you know what I know? A child, a child shivers in the cold, let us bring him silver and gold. Let us bring him all of ourselves."

Today's Prayer

Lord Jesus, I sing your praise this morning as I contemplate your tremendous holiness. Strengthen my desire for you today. I reach to you, my first love, that you might show me the heights and teach me your ways.

He Was Scum   DAY 2

> He was beaten, he was tortured, but he didn't say a word.
>
> Isaiah 53:7 THE MESSAGE

The servant grew up before God—a scrawny seedling, a scrubby plant in a parched field. There was nothing attractive about him, nothing to cause us to take a second look. He was looked down on and passed over, a man who suffered, who knew pain firsthand. One look at him and people turned away. We looked down on him, thought he was scum.

How many times have I lain awake at night, my mind scrolling through all the unattractive things in me, about me. The prophet Isaiah speaks to us all. He does not condemn us, nor does he thrust burning arrows of guilt into our guts. He tells us about a young boy who grew up, like we all do, before God. He suffered much ridicule, physical pain, and the disdain of his countrymen.

I can relate to this man. Though my suffering does not match his ultimate end, I find him approachable because he was hit in the mouth, because his beard was ripped out, because he was a second thought.

Jesus, the human, brings me peace. Not because he is King over all creation—and he most certainly is that. But because he entered into the *I and Thou* relationship. He stands across from me; he does not pummel me from above. Is there a deeper grace?

Today's Prayer

Lord Jesus, forgive me if your beatings bring me peace. You were despised and rejected, and I can relate. I can relate—that's really the heart of it. Thank you for relating. Thank you for peace.

Glory in the Highest DAY 3

Today's Prayer

Lord Jesus, today already my thoughts stray far from you.
Each day it seems I wake with good intentions only to find
myself in the corner of my heart, disgusted with myself.
And so I retreat into you, for you are my Word, my logos.

I hear the angels singing your praise. There they hover
over the fields and shepherds, pouring holy light upon the
sheep and countryside. I am with them, caught in awe,
afraid, for I am exposed in such incandescent light.

But your light cleanses as much as it exposes. You tell
me to fear not, and so my confidence rises, restored. Your
light and your glory speak to me, they tell me about you.
You desire all should come to you. You bring kindness to
us, those you created, those to whom you gave heavenly
purpose.

I stand, shaking no more, in your peace. But what is
this peace? Have I missed the world? Why am I standing
here now, feeling this wash of ease?

Your peace eases the heavy-laden hearts of darkness.
Your peace comes in light, and seeks the good of all hu-
mankind. The disgust in my heart crumbles, feeding the
ground where I stand. And in its place the flower of good-
ness rises. Nothing lies hidden from your goodness, from
your peace, from your love.

Glory to God in the highest,
And on earth peace, goodwill toward men!
Luke 2:14 NKJV

Indeed, glory to you, my God, in the highest.
Amen.

Close by Me Forever DAY 4

I will never leave you nor forsake you.

Hebrews 13:5

How can infinity fit into a manger? Why did the angels not overwhelm the animals with their light, frightening them to the point of death? What is it about this God of ours that draws him to human form—the very form he shaped from the dirt of the earth?

The incomprehensible poured into a knowable being, with skin, and hair, and a voice, and hands with which to touch that which he made—to be on the uncontrollable side of creation where love and hate and weather and death come at you.

God does not linger in the heavens, aloof to the cries of man. Indeed, he alighted unto our realm of death and bacon breakfasts and ate of it, all the way. The Christmas season boasts the bustle of shoppers and gift givers. And that is fine; Jesus came to give and to drink and to laugh. He has not outlawed joy. On the contrary, he is the author of joy. He is, at once, author, paper, and pen. Writing on the pulp of time with the etch of his life.

And in this etching he comes to me, he comes to you. He is not away, in a manger. Rather, he rests, close to you forever.

Today's Prayer

Lord Jesus, be near me, and I know you are. But today, as the winter sky lies low upon my heart, I need you ever near me—feeling your infinity, as close as swaddling clothes around my heart, as deep as the night, as brilliant as the day.

Shall I Play for You?   DAY 5

And when they saw it, they made known the saying that had been told them concerning this child. And all who heard it wondered at what the shepherds told them.

Luke 2:17–18

How does the news of Jesus' birth affect you? Me? "The Little Drummer Boy" remains one of my favorite carols. I love the intimacy of the little boy with the King whom he visits. He realizes his audience and at once desires to give something, anything. But alas, he has no gift to offer. He only carries a drum—and then it dawns on him. Shall I play for him?

Affirmed by Mary, he begins to play—all in attendance join in, the cows, the ox, and lamb. And so he played. But he didn't just *play*. He played his best for him.

We talk often of laying our burdens down at the cross. But what are we laying down in the manger? What do we have that is fit for this child King?

We come to Jesus with more than just burdens and darkness. We come to him with all of our selves. And when we do, he does not desire us to sheepishly sink into the shadows of the manger. No! He wants us to play—with everything we have within us.

What will you play for him today?

Today's Prayer

Lord Jesus, today I pray the words of Saint Augustine: "In the morning I shall stand in Your presence, and contemplate You; I shall for ever confess unto You. In the morning I shall stand in Your presence, and shall see the health of my countenance, my God, who also shall quicken our mortal bodies by the Spirit that dwells in us (Romans 8:11), because in mercy He was borne over our inner darksome and floating deep."[1]

You dwell in me, O Lord, and I pray today that I stand out from the shadows of this life and play for you—that your Holy Spirit may alight upon my soul and ignite it with a bold and holy confidence. I contemplate you, Lord Jesus, so that I may play for you.

Everlasting

Changeless in Changing Times   DAY 1

For I the Lord do not change.

Malachi 3:6

What comfort can I find today, in this sea of change? Daily the computers open, and load, and update, and are discarded. The new comes after the new arrives, and then something else new crests the horizon. We live in a time of obsolescence—things become obsolete. Do we?

But we are not like the things we purchase. We live and breathe and possess being. We're capable of loving and being loved. We stand in relation to one another and to God and so we last through the age, ebbing and flowing through this valley of shifting shadows.

Our comfort rests in the Unchanging One. He set the world into motion. He spoke, and through his words time ran forward, leaving its wake: the past. And yet on either side of time—its beginning and its coming end—the hands of God cup and hold

everything together. The Changeless One enlivening humans in
their changing times.

Consider Wordsworth's reflection on change:

> Truth fails not; but her outward forms that bear
> The longest date do melt like frosty rime,
> That in the morning whitened hill and plain
> And is no more; drop like the tower sublime
> Of yesterday, which royally did wear
> His crown of weeds, but could not even sustain
> Some casual shout that broke the silent air,
> Or the unimaginable touch of time.[1]

In all its glory and infamy, today will turn to tomorrow and
can do nothing to stop the churning. It wastes us at our core,
and yet we do not lose heart. For the God of Time guides us
into eternity—that timeless place of ceaseless glory and grace.

Today's Prayer

*Lord Jesus, my comfort rests in your unchanging ways.
Each day reminds me that I'm made for another world. I
see glimpses of glory, but they fade. Time marches on. But
you hold it all and you do not change. Be my unchanging
comfort today.*

Where Are You From?   DAY 2

Are you not from everlasting, O Lord my God, my Holy One?

Habakkuk 1:12

What does it mean to be "from everlasting"? On this winter's night, I walked along a muddy lane. It meandered out

into the open fields, a small wood to the west, Oxford sleeping quietly below, and the stars, oh the stars. What can we compare to everlasting? Certainly the heavens come close. And once beneath them in an open space, the expanse causes us—at least me—to feel an exhilarating uncomfortableness. The age of the stars, and their light, feels ancient and new. They are like the newborn child, at once a picture of innocence, freshness, and beginnings, and also representing the history of life itself, ancient and enduring.

God comes to us, dives down into time, from the everlasting. The place of evermore, the place we sense beneath the stars, the place we describe only with stories of fantasy—faeries and magic.

It is not the vastness of the everlasting that strikes us with sweet dread. Rather, it is that this God who approaches out of the great halls of the eternal is ours. The prophet says "my Holy One." Not a possession, but a partner, a friend.

Perhaps today you need to walk out into the fields, or the woods, or the mountains. Perhaps today you need to feel, to sense, some otherness—the otherness of "my Holy One." Take the time and walk. Get off your phone. Close the laptop. Shut down the tablet. The Everlasting awaits.

Today's Prayer

Lord Jesus, come to me, my Holy One. Wash me in the river of the everlasting so that I might glisten in heavenly glow. Here I am, walking through fields and over mountains, to you and with you into the infinite.

Lift Up My Soul   DAY 3

Today's Prayer
Today's prayer draws on Psalm 90:1–17.

Lord Jesus, what does it mean that you are my dwelling place?

And not just for me, but for all generations. My mind hurts as I ponder the everlasting that is you. And yet in your everlastingness I find temperance of mind—for wisdom ignites in the shadow of an eternal perspective.

Help me to number my days, Lord. When I realize that birth and death are bookends of my time here, it is wisdom that helps me make the most of the time you've given me. That time may be filled with great success, or daily drudgery, or the deepest pain. But it all falls under your reign.

Strengthen my earthly view with your view of eternity. A heavenly perspective is what I crave. I yearn for the steadfast love that you give daily, because it helps me see with your eyes; it helps me see past my light and momentary troubles.

Help me to live with contentment—with a constant prayer of thanksgiving. I pray for your everlastingness to fall upon me. I pray for your favor, and for you to establish the work of my hands. For though I am on my way to your everlasting, my heart desires to worship you with everything I do in this life.

Thy Kingdom, Come   DAY 4

His kingdom shall be an everlasting kingdom. . . .

Daniel 7:27

C. S. Lewis said the truth of our desire does not reveal any special thing about this world, but rather exposes the truth—that we were made for another world. Beyond the varying theologies surrounding what will happen at the end of all time, none of us can deny that something lies beyond the here and now. Whether it is brought to earth or extends into a heavenly dwelling does not matter.

What matters? Our reaction to this truth. How do we live now if we are made for an everlasting kingdom? What does it mean to hover in this life, to go on living, hoping for what lies beyond?

God did not reveal the everlasting to us so that we would disappear in the present and sit around waiting for what is to come. Hope of the everlasting moves us to bring the everlasting into the day-to-day. Jesus himself stands as our guide. He was everlasting given into the day-to-day to heal, to inspire, to forgive, to challenge, to bring peace, to bring a sword, to call out hypocrisy, to call out injustice, to love without measure, to offer grace with no end.

You and I walk through our days shining like beacons of the everlasting. That is our goal today. To shine on.

Today's Prayer
Lord Jesus, let your kingdom come. And let it come through me.

The Year's Yesterdays   DAY 5

Grace to you and peace from God our Father and the Lord Jesus Christ. . . . God, being rich in mercy, because of the great love with which he loved us, even when we were dead in our trespasses, made us alive together with Christ.

Ephesians 1:2, 2:4–5

Once we walked by the light of the world, which is no light at all—according to the prince of the air. Once we were children of wrath, but no more.

Grace now alights to us from the heavenlies, quickening our souls and bestowing the riches of his kindness. He showers us with this grace because he crafted us; as a poet to his poem, he carves out his thoughts with power and efficiency and weaves them into our souls.

He has brought us close to himself so that we are no longer castaways. We are *his.*

What joy, then, emerges from this life! Our afflictions, though they buffet us like a winter gale, do not overtake. For we have set our hopes on his strength. His might, mysterious, pulls us toward his horizon, past the temporal, past the day-to-day that hurts us so. Oh that we could capture this strength and sail to him more than we do—riding upon him *to* him.

This year's yesterdays end now. They bounce in our brains like fireflies in a jar, lighting up here and there helping us remember, remember, remember. In the remembering lies grace, and that grace allows us to forgive, to renew, and to grow again.

May we find comfort in the words of our Lord, may his precepts inspire us, and may his lovingkindness guide us in the years to come. May we walk in the Spirit so that we will not carry out the desires of the flesh.

Today's Prayer

Lord Jesus, bless me and keep me; make your face shine upon me and be gracious to me; lift up your countenance upon me, and give me your peace.[2]

Heavenly Peace and the Family of God

A Special Christmas Postscript

I remember how Christmas Eve felt when I was younger. Our church service marked the official beginning of all things tasty and gifty. Soon I would be sitting on the floor by the tree with my siblings, laughing, remembering, wrestling, and singing. That feeling never waned even when I became a man—I still look forward to this special service all year. Something about it epitomizes my church family.

I can see them: the faces arriving in cars, their mouths stretching ear to ear in silent, smiling discussion. The doors open and their jocund conversations spill out into the parking lot. Hands raise and heads bob—even the arrival teems with excitement.

A lightness permeates the foyer as the smiling faces bounce to and from other smiling faces, as if at any moment joy will explode from their ears. This constant teetering on the edge of jubilation can only come from a spirit biding its time. Anticipation abounds toward the love of the grand reveal: "Merry Christmas!" and the hand extends with gift and love and thanksgiving.

Mix the anticipation with a large group of people who meet several times each week to learn what it means to walk in the Way, to help one another, to serve the community. There is anticipation of gift-giving and receiving, anticipation of song-singing and reveling, anticipation of the Christ child. He came and will again come to us, the lowly and mild. A family expectant—that was my family of God, my church.

It was as if each year we lingered a bit longer on the final notes of "Silent Night," half-expecting Jesus himself to materialize in the candle glow. Some moments are best left to the imagination, but some moments are best expected, anticipated, even longed for.

I am, no doubt, painting quite the picture of the Christmas Eve service. My friend Jason says my poetic sensibilities in life are really just an overdeveloped sense of melodrama. He may be right, but if that is true, I am caught in the most exquisite melodrama ever penned. And of course one can never be too melodramatic about Christmas. It is the one time of year you and I return to sitting beneath a tree and, like a child, are expectant of the wonderful, the miraculous, the beautiful.

And yet, in later years it seems the Christmas Eve service has dimmed. It has become the church's big community opportunity, so we better not blow it. We better produce something great, even magnificent, all the bells and whistles—and, "Oh, can we get some bells and a sleigh riding into the manger and combine the myth with the True Myth? You know, Santa and Jesus together at last? Visitors would love that." It seems in our efforts to impress we have neglected the family business and allowed the silent night to turn rather loud.

What Others See

Imagine a family randomly attends your church on Christmas Eve. What do they see, experience, and feel?

Earlier that day Jack and Hillary discussed their Christmas Eve options.

"Where should we go for the Christmas Eve service?" yelled Hillary from the laundry room.

"I don't know, how about that big church with the massive parking lot?" said Jack as he poured another cup of coffee.

Hillary walked out of the laundry room still buttoning her new cardigan. "Yeah, I think that would be great. Sarah, from my book club, always raves about their music."

"Great, I don't really care, I just want to be able to get home to bed at a decent hour. Tomorrow is going to be nuts. Is it over? Is it New Year's?" said Jack half-joking, half-serious.

"For once, it seems like we agree."

As the family of five enters through the front door, they see Mr. Dennis leading the brass ensemble that is playing in the foyer—the musicians dressed like characters from a Dickens novel. More people gather and sip warm cider.

"Wow, this is pleasant—a bit of a surprise," says Jack to Hillary and the kids. They enter the sanctuary together, Mom herding the youngest away from the water fountain. An usher directs them to good seats close to the front.

A young teenager plays the piano and sings "Away in a Manger." She sounds like an angel. The lights dim and a gentle older man takes to the floor, not the stage. He welcomes everyone and talks about Christmas as a lad, how he loved it so much for the toys. Then he tells how the lad turned into a young man who found Jesus—the toys were fun, but Jesus was the best gift ever given.

"And tonight, it is because of the love of Jesus that *we* meet," says the solemn pastor. "To celebrate the birth of a King, that is why we've gathered together." Tears fill his eyes (as they often did every Sunday), and you can almost smell the stable and hear the sheep.

Jack looks at Hillary; she turns to him with tear-filled eyes, and smiles. They don't say a word but continue to listen while keeping their children occupied with crayons and iPhones.

"Sing with me 'Silent Night,'" the pastor says, and opens a hymnal.

The congregation sings while the deacons begin lighting candles. Each person offers their flame to their neighbor, and slowly the sanctuary glows with candlelight. The young family looks at all the glowing faces; everyone seems to be crying and laughing and looking out for one another—to see if so-and-so made it on this night of nights.

"Oh, there's Mr. Brunell," whispers the man standing next to Jack. "Hi, Mr. Brunell! Merry Christmas!" Mr. Brunell waves from across the aisle and flashes a Cheshire grin.

Jack leans in toward his wife. "I feel like we've snuck into a family gathering—everyone here seems to love each other so much. Kinda odd, but kinda perfect." Hillary does not turn, but keeps singing and nods her head—she's still crying.

"'Sleep in heavenly peace, sleep in heavenly peace . . .'" the song ends but the music continues to linger somehow, as if suspended by the candlelight.

The sanctuary empties, and the pastor with the gentle voice and teary eyes stands at the back and shakes hands with almost everyone, then quietly slips out with his wife. No one even notices.

But the visiting family notices.

Family Magic of a Silent Night

How does the story end? Does the visiting family return the following week to find out more about the programs this church has to offer? Do they enroll their kids in the school? That would, perhaps, make the most sense. But Jack and Hillary were not on the prowl for church programs. If you asked them, they would tell you they were not on the prowl for anything at all. You and I would probably answer the same way.

And yet we are prowling for something, you and me. And it is the same thing Jack and Hillary desire, only they do not know how to articulate it. My good friend Ed told me years ago that he began attending our church because he was invited to a Sunday evening service. I happened to be sharing my testimony that night. I was twenty years old and months earlier had been expelled from college. There I was, a pastor's kid, professing to everyone what I'd done, but more important, whom I had found in the process of my expulsion: Jesus.

Ed told me he wanted *that*. He wanted to belong to a group of people who valued transparency and truth and passion for Christ. Ed wanted to be part of the family of God.

And so let us suppose that Jack and Hillary return. They do so because something bigger than the gentle preacher leaked from his humble words. What is it behind that fierce gentleness that draws and pulls? It is the *mysterium tremendum*, the holiness of God. When our pride remains low enough, that holiness will leak.

Make no mistake, these final two weeks of the year hold magic in their days. A portal opens up in people where love and grace flow freely. The tension from the year loosens in most of us as we return to the foot of the tree, children once again. Or is that the foot of the cross, where you and I pray for our rebellion to be shaken from our souls?

In these days we make time for one another. Or is it Christ for whom we finally find the time?

In these days we sneak and eat and drink in a grand crescendo to Christmas Eve. Or is that Heaven's Table for which we are preparing, Christ awaiting his heavenly Bride?

In these days we find one another just when we need to, for forgiveness, for mercy, for the dying kind of love. Or is that what we find in those lingering notes of "Silent Night"?

Holy night indeed, and dripping with magic. Not the Santa magic—that is a topic for another essay—but the kind of magic that brings heaven down and captures it in candlelight. The kind that leaks from the words of a humble old pastor. The kind that leaks into Jack and Hillary without the aid of bells and whistles. The kind that helps us sleep on this night of nights in heavenly peace. Is it leaking in and through you?

I pray that it leaks.

Reflections

In these final weeks of the year, do your best to take time off. It is difficult, especially if you are used to a busy schedule, but you must allow time to pass and the winter days to bring the rest they are so good at bringing. Take time off, but do not fall into idleness. Reestablish the relationships you have neglected over the last few months, even year. Renew your commitment to your family, to your schoolwork, to your dreams.

Next, take an evening and retrace God's hand in your life this past year. Where has he been working? What patterns do you see arising? Might he be preparing you for something new, something more challenging, or something quite scary? Write down these "God-markers" in your journal (if you do not have a journal, purchase one). Maybe it looks like this:

> Last spring I'd been thinking of going back and finishing my degree. In May I met a professor randomly at Starbucks who told me about this new program at school. In July a friend of ours at church randomly suggested that I would make a good counselor—but in order to do that I'd need a degree.

After you have written out your God-markers, concentrate on your goals. If money were no object, if God gave you a free ride somewhere to do something, what would that be? What makes your heart jump when you consider it?

Finally, reflect on the piece above, about Jack and Hillary and Christmas Eve. What makes this year so special from your perspective? Gift-giving gets a bad reputation nowadays, but trace gift-giving back to Scripture. How can gift-giving be an excellent way to worship God and show appreciation for others? Reflect on your own church. Has it become too commercial? Do your leaders care too much about putting on the bells and whistles and not enough about cultivating a vibrant and thriving family of God?

Acknowledgments

Books demand time; in the writing and in the planning. And though much time is spent in quiet, staring at walls and writing in solitude, a community of people always surrounds, cheering. Here is my cheering crowd during this project.

I must first thank my Praxis family: Dave and Courtney Blanchard, Josh Kwan, Jon Hart, and George Veth. They gave me the space and encouragement to begin these reflections.

One of my closest friends, Jason Locy, encouraged me to compile these thoughts and cast a vision for the final book that inspired me go through with it. Thanks, Jason. "Hail, hail."

My great friend and agent Chris Ferebee—"Hey, I have this idea . . ."

A mentor and close friend Steve Graves has taught me what it means to have energy for others.

Special friends Brian and Mandy Miller—thank you for the encouraging emails, for reading, for pizza night, and for fires and dragon's milk.

Pastor Jon—thank you for Thursday mornings, truthful conversations, and continued friendship and guidance.

To the team at Bethany House, Jeff, Andy, Carra, and Tim, who believed in this project and worked so hard to help me see it realized, thank you.

My family—one mom, one dad, one mom-in-law, one dad-in-law, four siblings, two sisters-in-law, two brothers-in-law, sixteen grandchildren between us. What could be a better platform of love and inspiration?

My Fire family—you know who you are. Thank you.

My Starlight family—Holly and Jesse, for your unceasing love and always saying, "Do it, Tim. Go."

To Lacey and Joshua, for precious times of quiet worship, for always giving me truth in friendship, and for sharing these reflections at an early stage.

My Faerie family—my wife, Christine, for the whispering Oxford walks, and the pixies, Lyric, Brielle, and Zion, for setting the beautiful rhythms of our family.

To those who will read and think and pray, thank you. My prayers are with you and the application of God's Word into a living and vibrant theology.

Notes

1. Arthur Quiller-Couch, ed., *The Oxford Book of English Verse, 1250–1918* (Oxford: Clarendon Press, 1939), 294. Taken from the poem "Love."

Week 1: Joy

1. Søren Kierkegaard, *Christian Discourses,* "The Lily in the Field, the Bird of the Air," Walter Lowrie, trans. (Princeton, NJ: Princeton University Press, 1971).

2. A Celtic prayer from the Carmina Gadelica, a compendium of Celtic prayers, hymns, and poems handed down through oral tradition from the first Christians of Scotland and surrounding islands. Early Gaelic Book collection, http://digital .nls.uk/early-gaelic-book-collections/pageturner.cfm?id=78427452.

Week 2: Love

1. Søren Kierkegaard, et al., *Works of Love* (New York: HarperPerennial, 2009).

2. St. Augustine, *Saint Augustine Confessions* (Oxford: Oxford University Press, 1998), 201.

Week 3: Newness

1. Henri Nouwen, *The Way of the Heart* (New York: Ballantine, 1983), 11.

2. George MacDonald, *George MacDonald: An Anthology: 365 Readings* (New York: Simon & Schuster, 1996), 101.

3. F. F. Bruce, *The Epistles to the Colossians, to Philemon, and to the Ephesians* (Grand Rapids, MI: Eerdmans Publishing, 1984), 235.

Notes

Week 4: Thirst

1. Deuteronomy 4:29; 1 Chronicles 28:9; 2 Chronicles 15:2; Proverbs 8:17; and Isaiah 55:6.
2. A.W. Tozer, *Men Who Met God* (Camp Hill, PA: WingSpread Publishers, 1986).
3. C. S. Lewis and Pauline Baynes (illus.), *The Silver Chair* (London: Collins, 1998), 20–21.
4. Thomas à Kempis, *The Imitation of Christ*, trans. Aloysius Croft and Harold Bolton, Accordance electronic ed. (Altamonte Springs, FL: OakTree Software), n.p.

Week 6: Confession

1. Richard Baxter, *The Saints' Everlasting Rest, Select Works of Richard Baxter*, Accordance electronic ed. (Altamonte Springs, FL: OakTree Software, 2006), ii.

Week 7: Courage

1. Søren Kierkegaard, *The Sickness Unto Death* (New York: Penguin Books, 1989), 65.

Week 8: Work

1. Wendell Berry, from the essay "Christianity and the Survival of Creation," *Sex, Economy, Freedom, and Community* (New York: Pantheon Books, 1993), 104.

Week 9: Silence

1. *The Desert Fathers: Sayings of the Early Christian Monks* (New York: Penguin Books, 2003), 10.
2. Adapted from *Saint Augustine Confessions*, based on Matthew 4:23 and Psalm 102:3 (New York: Oxford University Press, 2008), 62.
3. This content on "Silence" was originally published by Timothy Willard and Jason Locy in *The Sound of Silence*, a free ebook resource provided exclusively through their website.

Week 10: Light

1. St. Augustine, *Saint Augustine Confessions* (Oxford: Oxford University Press, 1998), 276.
2. From 1 John 1:6–7 and Hebrews 1:3.

Week 11: Trust

1. Psalm 28:7

Week 12: The Long Pause, *I Want to Be Human*

1. C. S. Lewis, *An Experiment in Criticism* (Cambridge: Cambridge University Press), 138.

Notes

Week 13: Intimacy

1. Walt Whitman, *Leaves of Grass*, Bartleby: Great Books Online, www .bartleby.com/142/14.html.

Week 14: Anxiety

1. *The Screwtape Letters* by C. S. Lewis actually ran as a series of articles in the Anglican periodical *The Guardian* in 1941.
2. Luke 12:22–32 THE MESSAGE
3. Colossians 3:1–2 THE MESSAGE

Week 15: Surrender

1. Oswald Chambers, *My Utmost for His Highest*, "Total Surrender," http:// utmost.org/total-surrender/.
2. Ibid.

Week 17: Mystery

1. Hans Urs von Balthasar, *The Grain of Wheat: Aphorisms* (San Francisco: Ignatius Press, 1995), 20.
2. C. S. Lewis, *Reflections on the Psalms* (Orlando: Harcourt, 1986), 95.
3. Revelation 21:11
4. C. S. Lewis, *The Weight of Glory, and Other Addresses*, rev. ed. (New York: Macmillan, 1980), 7.
5. C. S. Lewis, *Mere Christianity* (New York: Touchstone, 1996), 121.

Week 18: Devotion

1. D. A. Carson, *The Gospel According to John* (Grand Rapids, MI: Eerdmans, 1991), 428.

Week 20: Kindness

1. Henri Nouwen, *The Way of the Heart* (New York: Ballantine Books, 2003), 20.
2. Ibid.

Week 22: Faithfulness

1. Dietrich Bonhoeffer, *The Cost of Discipleship* (New York: Simon & Schuster, 1995), 63.
2. Klaus Bockmuehl, *The Christian Way of Living* (Vancouver: Regent College Publishing, 1998), 35.

Week 23: Leadership

1. John Chrysostom, Homily 5 on 1 Corinthians, *Life and Practice of the Early Church*, edited by Steve McKinion (New York: NYU Press, 2001), 136.
2. I adapted Proverbs 4:23–27 for this prayer.

3. C. S. Lewis, "The Inner Ring," lecture presented at King's College, University of London, 1944, www.lewissociety.org/innerring.php.
4. Ibid.
5. Henri Nouwen, *In the Name of Jesus* (New York: Crossroad Publishing, 1989), 82.

Week 24: The Long Pause, *God of the Ridiculous*

1. Søren Kierkegaard, *Fear and Trembling: Dialectical Lyric by Johannes De Silentio* (Harmondsworth: Penguin, 1985 edition), 55.
2. Exerpts and ideas from this piece were drawn from Kierkegaard's *Fear and Trembling* and C. S. Lewis's essay "Man or Rabbit," which you can find in the collection *God in the Dock* (Eerdmans). I'd also like to thank the mystery writer of Hebrews for writing one of my favorite books of Holy Scripture.

Week 25: Prayer

1. Arthur Bennett, ed., "Morning Needs," *The Valley of Vision: A Collection of Puritan Prayers and Devotions* (Edinburgh: Banner of Truth Trust, 1975).
2. Andrew Murray, *Humility, Selected Works of Andrew Murray*, Accordance electronic ed. (Altamonte Springs, FL: OakTree Software, 2008), n.p. To make this small passage from Andrew Murray more personal, I have adapted it to read in the first person.
3. Edward M. Bounds, *The Necessity of Prayer*, Accordance electronic ed. (Altamonte Springs, FL: OakTree Software, 1999), n.p.
4. Ibid.

Week 26: Holy

1. A prayer credited to early church father John Chrysostom.

Week 27: Romance

1. C. S. Lewis, *The Four Loves* (New York: Harcourt Brace, 1960), 120–123.
2. Ibid., 33.

Week 28: Worth

1. 1 Peter 5:10–11
2. Psalm 17:1 KJV

Week 30: Worship

1. For more on the topic of what it means to encounter God in a worship setting, see Timothy Willard and R. Jason Locy, *Veneer: Living Deeply in a Surface Society* (Grand Rapids, MI: Zondervan, 2011).
2. John Chrysostom, Homily 5 on 1 Corinthians, *Life and Practice of the Early Church*, edited by Steve McKinion (New York: NYU Press, 2001), 136.

3. This reflection was originally sent to two dear friends who weekly serve the church through their leadership of musical worship.

Week 31: Longing

1. C. S. Lewis, *Perelandra* (New York: Scribner Classics, 1996), 38.

Week 32: Forgiveness

1. C. S. Lewis, "On Forgiveness" in *The Weight of Glory* (New York: HarperOne, 2009 edition), 182.
2. Adapted from portions of Psalm 86:5, Psalm 85:2, and Psalm 32:5 THE MESSAGE.

Week 33: Imagination

1. Corbin Scott Carnell, *Bright Shadow of Reality: Spiritual Longing in C. S. Lewis* (Grand Rapids, MI: Eerdmans, 1999), 72.

Week 34: Pain

1. From the poem "Dover Beach," by Matthew Arnold (1822–1888), http://www.poetryfoundation.org/poem/172844.
2. Ibid.
3. I am referring here to C. S. Lewis's famous description of pain as God's megaphone.

Week 35: Unity

1. C. S. Lewis, *God in the Dock* (Grand Rapids, MI: Eerdmans, 1970), 60.
2. C. S. Lewis, *Letters to Malcolm* (Orlando: Harcourt Brace, 1964), 16.
3. Michael Reeves, *Delighting in the Trinity* (Downer's Grove, IL: InterVarsity Press, 2012), 87–88. This little book is one everyone should read—it's short, intelligent, and beautifully written.
4. Psalm 91:4 NIV

Week 38: Dragons

1. Richard Baxter, *The Saints' Everlasting Rest, Select Works of Richard Baxter*, Accordance electronic ed. (Altamonte Springs: OakTree Software, 2006), ii.
2. Prayer adapted from Christian rock band Third Day with Lacey Mosley, "Born Again," by Mac Powell, 2008.
3. Frederick Buechner, *The Longing for Home: Recollections and Reflections* (San Francisco: HarperSanFrancisco, 1996), 7–10.

Week 39: Disappointment

1. C. S. Lewis, *The Screwtape Letters* (Uhrichsville, OH: Barbour and Co , 1990), 68–69.

Week 40: Shame

1. Brennan Manning, *The Importance of Being Foolish* (San Francisco: Harper-SanFrancisco, 2006), 127.

2. David Lose, "Misogyny, Moralism and the Woman at the Well," Huffington Post Religion, March 21, 2011, www.huffingtonpost.com/david-lose/misogyny -moralism-and-the_b_836753.html.

3. Ravi Zacharias, talk given at The Veritas Forum at UCLA, "Is Tolerance Intolerant?" January 16, 2013, http://www.mrctv.org/videos/shame-holy -and-pornography-men-listen.

4. C. S. Lewis, *The Problem of Pain* (New York: Simon & Schuster, 1996), 51.

5. Richard Foster, *Prayer* (New York: HarperCollins, 1992), 61.

6. Lewis, *The Problem of Pain* (New York: Simon & Schuster, 1996), 50.

Week 41: Strength

1. Dietrich Bonhoeffer, *The Cost of Discipleship* (New York: Touchstone, 1995), 157.

2. Deuteronomy 31:6 THE MESSAGE

3. Joshua 1:1–9 THE MESSAGE

4. Thomas Paine, "The American Crisis," pamphlet published December 1776, http://memory.loc.gov/cgi-bin/query/r?ammem/rbpe:@field%28DOCID+@ lit%28rbpe03902300%29%29.

Week 42: Passion

1. Richard J. Foster, *Prayer: Finding the Heart's True Home* (London: Hodder & Stoughton, 2008), 69.

2. Verses taken from Exodus 3:5–6.

3. Psalm 6:4, 6–7 NIV.

Week 44: Beauty

1. Cyril Charles Richardson, et. al., *Early Christian Fathers* (Louisville: Westminster John Knox Press, 2006), 216–218.

2. Oswald Chambers, *My Utmost for His Highest* (Uhrichsville, OH: Barbour, 2007), November 2 reading.

Week 45: Eclipse

1. From George MacDonald's *The Diary of an Old Soul* (Minneapolis: Augsburg Fortress, 1994), Day 3.

Week 46: Anticipation

1. "Definitions for Medieval Christian Liturgy: *Sanctus*," http://www.yale.edu/ adhoc/research_resources/liturgy/d_sanctus.html.

Week 47: Heights

1. Søren Kierkegaard, *The Sickness Unto Death* (New York: Penguin Books, 1989), 74.

Week 48: The Long Pause, *The Color Green*

1. Rich Mullins, "The Color Green," 1993. BMG Songs, Inc.

Week 49: Jesus

1. St. Augustine, *Confessions,* Book XIII, Chapter XIV.

Week 50: Everlasting

1. William Wordsworth, *Poetical Works [of] Wordsworth*, "Mutability" (London: Oxford University Press, 1969), 353.

2. Portions from today's reflection were taken from some of my own paraphrasing from the following passages: Ephesians 1 and 2; 2 Corinthians 1; Numbers 6; and Galatians 5:16.

Even Deeper

As I noted in the introduction, "God Rhythms," I do not find it helpful to clutter my devotional reading with myriad writers and books. I like to dive deep into a handful of writers. So I thought I might include a few of my favorite resources. You can also reference the Notes section if you are interested in any particular source I used in the book.

Of course, nothing can substitute for in-depth Bible study, but I pray that some of these materials might further enrich your times of reflection and prayer.

C. S. Lewis, *Reflections on the Psalms*

_____. *The Screwtape Letters*

_____. "The Weight of Glory"

_____. "The Trouble With X"

_____. *George MacDonald: An Anthology*

_____. *A Grief Observed*

George MacDonald, *Diary of an Old Soul*

Søren Kierkegaard, *Works of Love*
_____. *Christian Discourses*
_____. *Fear and Trembling*

St. Augustine, *Confessions*

A Book of Puritan Prayers, *The Valley of Vision*

Chuck Swindoll, *Intimacy With the Almighty*
_____. *So You Want to Be Like Christ?*

Thomas à Kempis, *Imitation of Christ*

Kenneth Boa, *Face to Face*

About the Author

Timothy Willard serves as Spiritual Director for the Praxis Nonprofit Accelerator and coauthored the critically acclaimed book *Veneer: Living Deeply in a Surface Society.* When he's not scratching poetry, chasing the scholar's craft, or carving trails on his mountain bike, he enjoys making up faerie stories about the English countryside for his wife and three pixie daughters.

Though Timothy, like most writers, loves Hemingway, he does not understand why most writers fear using language. Given the choice between Joyce or Hemingway, Timothy chooses the former. He abhors "ly" words even though he was forced to use them in this manuscript. To Timothy, writing is both a joy and an act of commitment. It is the hard work, but refreshingly so.

Timothy has spoken at national conferences such as the Q Conference, Catalyst Conference, and Focus on the Family's Justice Conference, but his favorite audience is the one he puts to bed each night with stories he's trying to stack into a couple of children's books.

Timothy holds a master's degree from Gordon-Conwell Theological Seminary and is reading for a PhD in Theology at King's College London under the supervision of renowned theologian and apologist Alister McGrath.

Timothy would love to connect with you.
Find him at his website: **www.timothywillard.com**